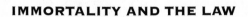

IMMORTALITY AND THE LAW

IMMORTALITY AND THE LAW

The Rising Power of the American Dead

Ray D. Madoff

Yale UNIVERSITY PRESS

New Haven & London

Published with assistance from the Mary Cady Tew Memorial Fund.

Set in type by Technologies 'N Typography. Printed in the United States of America by Sheridan Books.

Library of Congress Cataloging-in-Publication Data
Madoff, Ray D.
Immortality and the law : the rising power of the American dead /
Ray D. Madoff.
     p. cm.
Includes bibliographical references and index.
ISBN 978-0-300-12184-1 (clothbound : alk. paper)
1. Estate planning—United States.   2. Perpetuities—United States.
3. Defamation of the dead—United States.   I. Title.
KF750.M328 2010
346.7305'2—dc22   2009045472

A catalogue record for this book is available from the British Library.

This paper meets the requirements of ANSI/NISO Z39.48-1992 (Permanence of Paper).

10 9 8 7 6 5 4 3 2 1

To David, Gabriel, Jesse, and Amelia Nicholas and in memory of my parents, Irving and Janice Madoff

CONTENTS

ACKNOWLEDGMENTS

I am deeply indebted to the many people who helped transform this book from an idea to a reality. I appreciate all the support I received from my colleagues at Boston College Law School as well as generous financial support from the Boston College Law School Fund and the Darald and Juliet Libby Fund.

This project would be a pale version of itself if not for the thoughtful comments and assistance of the following individuals: Buzzy Baron, Paulo Barrozo, Mary Bilder, John Bowman, Al Brophy, Mike Cassidy, Allison Chernow, Betsy Foote, Gigi Georges, Brett Goldberg, Phyllis Goldfarb, Theresa Hammond, Frank Herrmann, Greg Kalscheur, Sanford Katz, Marjorie Kornhauser, Debi Korzenik, Joe Liu, Emily Madoff, Harriet Madoff, Robbie Madoff, Judy McMorrow, Eve Minkoff, Julia Nourok, David Olson, Michael Orey, Judy Perlman, Vlad Perju, Jim Repetti, Diane Ring, Amedeo Santosuosso, Amy Schwartz, Avi Soifer, Judy Tracy, Gerhard Vorwold, and Fred Yen. It has also benefitted from the excellent research assistance of Jackie Asadorian, Simon Burce, Annette Eaton, Jeanne Semivan, and Tao Eun Seo.

I owe special thanks to Michael O'Malley, my editor at Yale University Press, who supported this project from its infancy and was steadfast by my side through all of its varied iterations. I will miss our regular phone conversations. I also appreciate the work of my superb manuscript editor, Laura Jones Dooley.

Finally, nothing would be possible without the love and support of my rock, my husband, Dave Nicholas, and the joy provided by our children, Gabe, Jesse, and Amelia. It is to them, and in memory of my wonderful parents—Janice and Irving Madoff—that I dedicate this book.

IMMORTALITY AND THE LAW

INTRODUCTION: THE LAW OF THE DEAD

In this age in which more information is known and easily accessible by the masses than ever before in history, there is one subject about which we are as ignorant as our forebears, and that is death. For most of us, our ignorance about death is a fact of life. We either accept death's mystery or ignore its inevitability. Our legal system, however, cannot afford these philosophical or psychological luxuries. The law is constantly being asked to address real issues involving the dead: Are people harmed when someone tells lies about them after death? To what extent do people have an interest in what happens to their body after death? What about their property? For each of these questions—and more—the law has been required to provide answers.

Through history and around the world, societies have taken different approaches to the legal treatment of the dead. In some cases, people's legal interests have been extinguished along with their corporal existence. In other cases, the law has continued to protect the interests of the deceased, thereby providing them with a form of virtual immortality.

American law has taken its own uniquely American approach to the law of the dead, colored in recent years by the distinct imprint of the baby boom generation. This generation is becoming the largest population of elderly in the history of the United States. Just as they have left their mark on other areas of American society at every stage of their lives, baby boomers are transforming the legal landscape to claim more of the country's riches for themselves—the future dead of America. This book tracks this transformation.

The Law of the Dead—It's Everywhere

Legal issues involving the interests of the dead come up in surprisingly numerous ways and contexts. Although we most commonly think of the dead as exercising legal rights by leaving instructions regarding the disposition of their property, legal issues of the dead also arise regarding the control of a person's body, reputation, and artistic creations.

At one time, dead bodies were primarily something to be buried. Legal questions regarding dead bodies were generally limited to determining who among the living was responsible for interment. Today we are presented with many more options than past generations regarding the final use and disposition of our bodies. This range of possibilities raises many more legal questions. Can people make legally enforceable decisions about whether their body is buried or cremated, dissected for scientific study, harvested for organ transplants, or plasticized for display in traveling exhibits?

More issues are raised by reproductive matter. It is now a relatively simple procedure to exhume sperm from a dead man. It may soon be possible to remove viable eggs from dead women. Do people have a legal right to control whether their eggs or sperm are exhumed after death for posthumous child production? If children are posthumously conceived, should they be treated as offspring of the deceased "parent"?

Cryonics raises some of the most vexing problems regarding the legal treatment of dead bodies because there is vast disagreement as to its viability. Some people believe that the technology will eventually be available and view cryonics as offering the best opportunity for people finally to be able to transcend death. Others see cryonics as a pipe dream and the cryonics industry as charlatanism at its worst, taking advantage of people at their most vulnerable time of life. Will the law outlaw, tolerate, or encourage cryonics? If allowed, who will decide whether a person's body will be frozen for possible reanimation? If cryonics were to work, would the newly defrosted person be treated as the same person who died or as a new individual?

Reputational interests raise another set of questions. Some aspects of reputation lie firmly outside the law. If, for example, a friend divulges our most embarrassing secrets, the law generally does not get involved. The law does step in, however, to safeguard reputations in cases of defamation and invasions of privacy. Will these protections extend beyond death?

A person's artistic creations, name, and image lie somewhere between property and reputational interests. During a person's lifetime, the legal doctrines of copyright, right of publicity, and moral rights allow people to control the exploitation of their works. What about after death? Can artists continue to exert control over what happens to their creations? Through computers, actors' images can be manipulated such that they can continue to star in new movies long after death. Can an actor leave instructions that control the extent that this will be allowed to happen?

Even the question regarding control of property at death is knottier then it initially appears. Although American law provides explicit protections for people to be able to transmit their property at death, there is a distinction between directing who receives property and imposing long-term controls over that property.

Trusts allow people to leave instructions on the use and disposition of their property. They are commonly established to benefit particular individuals or to promote charitable or other purposes. Their appeal and potential power lies, in part, in the fact that they can be drafted to last long after the lives of the settlor and all the beneficiaries living at the time the trust is created. Yet although the trust mechanism creates the *possibility* of long-term posthumous control, the law must decide the extent to which this protracted control will be allowed. For example, the law must decide whether there will be time limitations on trusts. Can a person set money aside for his or her great-great-great-great-great grandchildren (expected to be born sometime in the twenty-third century)? In addition to duration, there is the question as to the extent to which the law will allow posthumous meddling by enforcing trust provisions that are designed to encourage (or even coerce) certain behavior by the beneficiaries after the settlor has died. For example, will the courts enforce a trust provision that a beneficiary will inherit only if he or she pursues a particular career or marries someone of the same faith? What if the contingencies of the trust require him or her to practice a particular religion or to refrain from marriage altogether? What if it requires the beneficiary to commit a crime in order to inherit?

Trusts also can be used as mechanisms to further particular causes. For example, through a trust a person might direct that his property be used to eradicate diabetes or promote martial arts (or, more perversely, to eradicate martial arts or promote diabetes). Although during life there is essentially no limit on the types of purposes people can support, after death, they are entirely dependent on the law's recognition and enforcement to make these things happen. The law must consider and adopt rules regarding how much latitude it will give people in committing their property to a purpose. Can property be set aside for any purpose at all? Can people order the destruction of their property ("I can't stand the thought of anyone else enjoying my Fabergé eggs or Rembrandt paintings")? Can these trusts last forever, or will a time limit be imposed? What happens if the circumstances change and the purpose of the trust no longer makes sense?

For each of these questions, and more, the law is called upon for answers.

Conceptions of Death and the Law

The question of how the law should treat interests of the dead is affected at least in part by our understanding of what it means to be dead. For example, if we believed—as did many who lived in ancient Greece— that the dead must pay a ferryman to be carried across a river to the afterlife, then we would likely find it appropriate for the law to ensure that the dead were buried with worldly goods such as coins (the Greeks stored them in the mouth for safekeeping) so that the deceased would not be left to beg or borrow his or her way to the other side. Alternatively, if we believed that the dead could "see" what was happening among the living (as the afterlife is often depicted in American movies and literature), then we might find it appropriate for the law to continue to provide many of the same protections for the dead that it does for the living so as to not hurt people's feelings.[1]

What if the starting point is—as many people believe—that death marks the end of all conscious existence? This raises the question: If death marks the end of conscious existence, shouldn't it also mark the end of legal existence? Societies take this position with respect to voting. No matter how committed people may be to a particular party or candidate during their life, the law does not allow them to cast ballots for elections occurring after their death. The justification for this rule seems self-evident: we are skeptical about people's ability to make good decisions for the future when they are limited in their knowledge to the world of the present. It seems inappropriate, moreover, to give decision-making authority to people who will not be around to enjoy the benefits or suffer the consequences of their decisions.

This was an early American value, expressed by no less than Thomas Jefferson, who frequently warned against allowing the wishes of the dead to prevail over those of the living:

> That our Creator made the earth for the use of the living and not of [the] dead; that those who exist not can have no use nor right in it, no authority or power over it, that one generation of men cannot foreclose or burthen its use to another, which comes to it in its own right and by the same divine beneficence; that a preceding generation cannot bind a succeeding one by its laws or contracts; these are axioms so self evident that no explanations can make them plainer: for he is not to be reasoned with who says that non-existence can control existence or that nothing can move something.[2]

And yet today there are many situations where American law, as well as the law of other countries, recognizes interests of the dead, enforces their decisions, and allows them to bind the living.

Patterns and Trends in American Law of the Dead

The legal issues involving interests of the dead have arisen and developed within different substantive corners of American law, including torts, property, criminal law, evidence, intellectual property, privacy, and tax. As such, scant attention has been paid to the cumulative picture of the law of the dead, and little effort has gone into understanding its far-reaching implications.[3] By wending our way through these different corners and culling the law of the dead, however, we can observe patterns that would otherwise remain undetected.

This book shines a light on the cumulative picture of the law of the dead and, in so doing, explores two themes in depth. The first is that American law has its own distinct approach to the treatment of interests of the dead that differs significantly from that taken by other countries. These differences reflect fundamental value choices, because the allocation of rights to the dead invariably affects the resources available to the living. The second theme is the distinct and recently accelerating trend in American law to grant greater and greater rights to the dead. These rights have been granted with little attention paid to the costs imposed on the living.

The defining features of American law of the dead in the twenty-first century are as follows:

- Americans exert significant control over property at death. Family members generally have no claim over their deceased relatives' property. Moreover, Americans are largely free to impose whatever conditions they want, and their plans can often be imposed for as long as they want, even in perpetuity.
- American law provides no protections for reputational interests after death. Claims for defamation and invasion of privacy do not apply once a person is no longer living.
- American law has an uneasy relationship with control over the body. The foundational principle is that people do not own their bodies and thus have no enforceable rights to control their bodies after death. In recent years, however, this has been complicated owing to the increased need for bodies for transplant and medical study.

The American legal system has made choices regarding rights of the dead that differ significantly from those made by other countries. Most distinctly, whereas the United States grants broad rights to people to control their property after death, virtually every other country in the world limits these rights in a number of important ways. First, most countries limit the ability of people to direct their property after death by imposing systems of forced succession, which require that a large portion of their property (commonly up to 80 percent) be given to family members in designated shares. Even those countries that lack a formal system for family succession nonetheless grant courts the power to diverge from the instructions left in a person's will in order to effectuate a fairer distribution of a person's estate. This is unlike American law, where freedom of testation is paramount and the courts have no power to deviate from a person's will.

A second distinction involves the ability to impose long-term controls over property. Whereas the United States facilitates long-term control of property through the device of the trust, most other countries do not recognize trusts. Even in those countries that do recognize trusts, after the settlor of the trust has died, the living beneficiaries are generally given far greater control over the property than under American law. For example, in the United Kingdom any of the living beneficiaries of a trust can break a trust, regardless of the settlor's intent. This is in contrast to the United States, where beneficiaries have no right to break a trust if the settlor's purpose can still be fulfilled.

A third area where American law differs substantially from the law of other countries concerns reputation. Whereas American law provides essentially no protection for a person's reputation after death, other countries take a very different approach. A number of European countries are much more concerned with the dignity of the dead. They often have governmental organizations that are specifically charged with protecting individuals' privacy and reputational interests after death. Moreover, other countries also grant artists much broader posthumous protections over their work and name than are given in the United States.

American law regarding interests of the dead has changed over time, and this change has a pattern: American law has moved over the years to grant more rights to the dead. This change has been particularly notable in terms of Americans' ability to exert control over their property after death. Dynasty trusts, charitable trusts, copyright law, and the right of publicity are all areas where the dead have been given increasingly greater rights over the course of American history. The rights of the dead have flourished while little attention has been paid to the costs imposed on the living.

Dynasty trusts provide a recent mechanism through which people can exert their wishes long after they have died. For centuries, the law placed a limit of approximately ninety years for the duration of noncharitable trusts. It was considered bad policy to allow people to exert control for a period longer than the lives of those living at the time of the creation of the trust, plus the term of minority for the next generation. This ninety-year limitation was accomplished through the arcane Rule against Perpetuities, which required all interests in trusts "to vest or fail within lives in being plus 21 years." Beginning in the late twentieth century, however, a number of states began repealing the Rule against Perpetuities. The banking industry lobbied for this transformation because it facilitated the marketing of a tax savings device known as the dynasty trust and resulted in the influx of dollars to banks operating in jurisdictions with this favorable legislation. Today, Americans have the ability to set property aside for the use of their heirs in perpetuity. Because trust law is so flexible, these dynasty trusts can also shield the beneficiaries from liability to creditors, including victims of a beneficiary's tortious acts. Because of their recent vintage, the social costs of dynasty trusts have not yet been felt. The result of these trusts, however, will be the creation of new societal divisions between those who are beneficiaries of these tax-free, judgment-proof, long-term trusts, and the rest of society.

In addition to the potential harm to society, these dynasty trusts can harm the beneficiaries themselves. Many wealthy people, including Andrew Carnegie and Warren Buffet, believe that it is not in their children's best interest for them to be given so much wealth that they don't need to work. As Carnegie said: "It is no longer questionable that great sums bequeathed oftener work more for the injury than for the good of the recipients." And yet, dynasty trusts take this decision-making authority away from parents because the ancestor settling the trust decides how much wealth their descendants will get at each generation.

Charitable trusts provide another powerful mechanism for people to live on after death. In a charitable trust, a person directs that his or her property be devoted to a particular charitable purpose. Ford, MacArthur, Rockefeller, Pulitzer, Nobel, and Olin are all names known to us today because these people left money in eponymous charitable trusts. Given their ubiquity, it might be hard to believe that charitable trusts were not allowed under American law throughout most of the nineteenth century.

It was thought to be poor policy to allow individuals to create their own perpetual entities devoted to whatever purpose they thought best. Beginning in the twentieth century, however, the perpetual private charitable trust became not only tolerated but favored in the law and subsidized by the government through the tax code. Charitable giving is undeniably able to accomplish substantial good, but the subsidy for individual charitable giving means that fewer resources are available for governmental programs. Moreover, our current laws give considerable deference to maintaining these charitable trusts in perpetuity. Unfortunately, current law does nothing to address issues of waste that are all too prevalent in perpetual charitable entities.

Copyright law is yet another area where American law has moved to grant more rights to the dead. Copyright law was originally established to provide a short-term monopoly for a person's creative works, after which time the creation would become part of the public domain. The original copyright term was fourteen years, with the possibility of renewal for one more fourteen-year term if the holder was still living. Thomas Jefferson chose this term based on actuarial calculations because he wanted the term to last no longer than the life of the original holder. Over the years, however, as copyrights have grown in value and as they have become important business assets, the copyright statute has been revised numerous times, consistently lengthening the term for copyright protection. Today, rather than lasting for the life of the creator, copyright protection now lasts until seventy years after the death of the creator. Because of these changes, a work created today will likely not be available for general consumption until the middle of the next century.

Although this copyright extension has produced more value for private owners, it has come at a significant cost to society. The increase in copyright protection both limits public access to original works and inhibits the creation of new works that build on the originals. The harm caused by this extension of copyright is made even greater by the breadth of copyright protection. Many were surprised when the family of Martin Luther King, Jr., sued *USA Today* for publishing and CBS for broadcasting the "I Have a Dream" speech without first paying the family. They were even more surprised when the family won. Since then the family has exerted a stranglehold on King's image and words. Indeed even the foundation that is building a memorial to Dr. King on the National Mall was required to pay the family eight hundred thousand dollars for the use of his words and image.[4] The enforcement of these rights is even more aggressive when they are owned by corporate entities that can afford large legal departments to enforce their interests.

The right of publicity is a final area where in recent years the dead have acquired rights that never before existed under American law. The right of publicity is the right of an individual to control the commercial value of her name, image, and likeness. The right of publicity has been used by the singer Bette Midler to stop a car company from using a singer in a commercial who sang in a style similar to Midler and by Jacqueline Kennedy Onassis to stop an advertiser from using an Onassis look-alike.

The right of publicity was born in the early twentieth century. When it was first recognized under the law, its protections were explicitly limited to the life of the person. Beginning in the 1950s, however, American law began to treat the right of publicity as a property (as opposed to personal) interest that could be freely marketed. Shortly thereafter, states began adopting statutes allowing the right of publicity to survive death. Although states differ in their approach, the most common duration of protection is fifty years after death. However, Indiana, home of CMG Worldwide, one of the largest corporate holders of rights of publicity, has a statute that grants protection for one hundred years. Tennessee, home of Elvis Presley, has enacted a statute that has the power to protect a person's right of publicity in perpetuity. Other states are under similar pressure to expand the duration of their rights of publicity.

The extension of the right of publicity has created value for heirs and the corporate entities that frequently own these interests. This, too, comes at a cost, however. Almost every celebrity owes at least part of his or her identity to celebrities of the past (for example, Mae West, Jean Harlow, Marilyn Monroe, and Madonna are all incarnations of the forthright sexual blonde). By granting current celebrities and their heirs exclusive control over these identities, we deny their beneficial use to future generations of would-be celebrities.

The rights of the American dead have multiplied over the years. This growth of rights has undoubtedly provided economic and perhaps even psychological benefits to some. But for society, these new rights involve a transfer of resources and their control away from the living. Societies at different times have made different decisions regarding the legal rights of the dead. By studying these decisions, we can gain important insights into a society's understanding of death, as well as what it truly values for the living.

1

CONTROLLING THE BODY

Nothing is more quintessentially "ours" than our bodies. We may have nothing in the world, but we all have a body in which we live.

During life, the law recognizes a right to control our bodies in a number of ways. First and foremost, under American law, everybody owns his or her own body. Since the abolition of slavery, no person can be said to own another.[1] In addition, the law protects people's bodies from harm by others. If someone hurts your body intentionally, he or she is subject to criminal punishment. If a person does not intend to hurt you but does so anyway through reckless or negligent actions, she or he can be held legally responsible for any damage caused to your body. Recognition of a fundamental right to control one's body provides the basis on which people can refuse medical treatment—even if that refusal results in death. The right to control reproduction through the use of birth control and sometimes abortion is also tied to personal bodily integrity.

To be sure, there are limits on what we can do with our bodies. In particular, prostitution and the sale of organs or bodies for reproductive purposes are against the law. Yet these prohibitions are most accurately described as prohibitions on the receipt of money for particular purposes rather than as prohibitions on the use of our bodies. In fact, each of these activities—sex, carrying another person's baby, or giving organs to another person—can all be done legally so long as no money is exchanged in the transaction.

What happens to this right to control our bodies after death? Certainly a body after death is very different from a living human being. It is no longer capable of actions or thoughts; unless treated, it quickly decomposes. Even after death, however, human bodies can serve many important functions, and decisions about dead bodies are critical to a lot of people. In particular, human bodies can be used for the following purposes:

- As a source of psychological comfort to survivors who may find closure in knowing where the body is and in the knowledge that it has been handled appropriately;
- In religious preparations for the afterlife of the deceased;
- As a source of organs for others;
- In autopsies, as a source of information regarding possible criminal activity or to gather important health information for surviving relatives;
- As a source of genetic material that can used for posthumous procreation;
- For medical research and the education of medical students;
- In traveling exhibits, such as Body World;
- To provide another chance at life through cryonics;
- For necrophilia; and
- For cannibalism.

Who makes the decisions regarding the treatment of a body after death? Who decides if a person's body is cremated or buried in a religious ceremony, preserved cryonically for future "defrosting" or donated to science for disassembling into its component parts? To what extent can a person control what happens to his or her body after death, the way that he or she can during life?

Throughout history, the most powerful individuals, from King Tutankhamen to Napoleon Bonaparte, have often been able to direct what happens to their bodies after death. Yet no matter how powerful someone is in his or her own time, their wishes remain subject to the whims of future generations. Thus, although Vladimir Lenin's body has been lying in state in Moscow's Red Square since his death in 1924, since the fall of Communism there has been talk of interring the body.[2]

What about the average person? To what extent does she control what happens to her body after death? On an anecdotal level, it appears that people have a great deal of control, for there are many examples in which an individual's idiosyncratic requests regarding the disposition of his or her remains is respected. Consider the following:

- Jeremy Bentham, the English philosopher and father of Utilitarianism, requested that his body be stuffed and displayed in a glass case at the University of London. It still sits there today.[3]
- Sandra West, a wealthy Beverly Hills socialite, asked that she be buried in her 1964 baby blue Ferrari dressed in a lace nightgown and with the "seat slanted comfortably." She was buried as requested in a cemetery in San Antonio, Texas.[4]
- The ashes of Timothy Leary, psychologist, writer, and advocate of psychedelic drug use, were shot into space aboard a rocket carrying the remains of twenty-four other people, including Gene Roddenberry, the creator of *Star Trek*.
- Eugene Merle Shoemaker, one of the founders of the field of planetary science, is buried on the moon.
- Hunter S. Thompson, author and journalist, let it be known that his last wish was for his ashes to be blasted from a cannon while his friends raised their glasses in a toast. His wish was carried out six months after his suicide, when friends gathered at his home near Aspen, Colorado. Accompanied by red, white, blue, and green fireworks, Thompson's ashes were blasted into the sky from the top of a 153-foot tower.[5]
- Charlie Whitmore, a lifelong hiker and outdoorsman, requested that his ashes be spread on 315 peaks in southern Arizona; the *New York Times* reported that as of 2006, Whitmore's remains had been spread on 176 peaks and that the hikers from his club were working on the remaining 139.[6]

These stories suggest that we each have the right to control what happens to our bodies after death. But this conclusion is not necessarily true, and just as there are cases where idiosyncratic burial requests are granted, there are also numerous cases where a person's wishes regarding the disposition of his or her body are essentially ignored. Consider the following:

- Albert Einstein, the most famous scientist of the twentieth century, did not donate his body to science. Instead, he expressed the wish that his body be cremated: "I want to be cremated so that people won't come to worship at my bones." When Einstein died, his body was cremated . . . but not all of it. Before cremation, the pathologist who conducted the autopsy on Einstein's body removed and kept his brain. Without any previous consent from Einstein or his family, the pathologist stored sections of Einstein's brain in cardboard boxes and glass jars and distributed pieces to various scientists over the years for study. Today parts of Einstein's brain are located in Lawrence, Kansas, and at the University of California at Berkeley, as well as in Japan, Australia, and Germany.[7]

- Steven Brotherton had an aversion to organ transplants. After his body was found "pulseless" in an automobile, it was brought to the hospital. His wife declined a request to make an anatomical gift because of her husband's stated views. Nonetheless, while the body was being subjected to autopsy, the coroner permitted Brotherton's corneas to be removed and delivered to an eye bank for future transplant.

- Ted Williams, the legendary baseball player, explicitly provided in the first paragraph of his will: "I direct that my remains be cremated and my ashes sprinkled at sea off the coast of Florida where the water is very deep." Nonetheless, when he died, rather than being cremated and sprinkled at sea, the baseball legend's body was flown to Arizona, where his head and body are currently being stored in separate tanks of liquid nitrogen in a state of cryonic suspension.

- Franklin Delano Roosevelt left detailed instructions that he wished to be buried in a plain pine casket placed in an unlined grave. He did not want any pomp and circumstance associated with his funeral. Instead, however, FDR was buried in an expensive casket in a lined grave following a state funeral with a great deal of ceremony.[8]

- Grace Metalious, the author of the blockbuster 1950s novel *Peyton Place,* left specific instructions about the disposition of her body after death. She instructed in her will that she wanted "no funeral services [to] be held for me, and that my body be given [to] the Dartmouth School of Medicine, for the purpose of experimentation in the interest of medical science." To ensure that her wishes be carried out, she also provided a backup plan: "If Dartmouth does not accept then to Harvard Medical School." Metalious's family, however, had other plans.

At the time of her death, her husband and children objected to this provision. Undoubtedly to avoid controversy, the medical schools declined to accept her body. The family also had other ideas about a funeral and began planning one. Although the executor of Metalious's estate tried to get a court to stop the funeral on the grounds that it was against her wishes, the court refused the request and allowed a funeral service to take place.[9]

Development of the Law of the Body: Foundational Rules

Before the mid-nineteenth century, a corpse was of little value, and its possible uses were few. Indeed, a corpse was a liability, because it needed to be disposed of in a way that did not create a public health risk. One judge described the challenge of creating laws around the corpse as follows:

> A corpse in some respects is the strangest thing on earth. A man who but yesterday breathed and thought and walked among us has passed away. Something has gone. The body is left still and cold, and is all that is visible to mortal eye of the man we knew. Around it cling love and memory. Beyond it may reach hope. It must be laid away. And the law—that rule of action which touches all human things—must touch also this thing of death.[10]

Early legal rules applicable to corpses were relatively straightforward. They involved establishing who controlled the disposition of the body, setting standards for proper treatment of the body after death, and, most surprisingly to people today, imposing punishment on a body for crimes of the decedent.

Controlling Disposition of the Body: No Property Interest in Your Body

The most important rule regarding controlling bodies after death was one that the United States inherited from the common law of England, that is, the rule that a person does not have a property interest in his or her own body after death. The principle of common law is "corpus nullius in bonis," the body belongs to no one.[11]

The decision most often cited for this proposition is the English case, *Williams v. Williams*.[12] In that case, a man by the name of Henry Crookenden—an early advocate of cremation—provided in his will that on his death, his body was to be given to his friend Eliza Williams "to be dealt with in the manner provided for in a letter to her." In this letter, he laid out his wishes with specificity: he wanted his body burned under a pile of wood and the remains stored in a particular Wedgwood vase that Crookenden had conveniently provided to Williams through his will.

When Crookenden died, rather than following the wishes laid out in his will, his family buried him with the rites of the Roman Catholic Church. Eliza Williams tried to enforce the provisions of the will. In refusing her request, however, the court ruled that "there can be no property in a dead body": "[A] man cannot by will dispose of his dead body. If there be no property in a dead body it is impossible that by will or any other instrument the body can be disposed of."[13]

Although it was undoubtedly affected by the decedent's avant-garde choice of burial, the court went out of its way to state that its decision had much broader applicability: "If the purpose had merely been for burial in a particular cemetery, which would be entirely according to the law of this country, that would not make the direction to deliver the body to someone who was not an executor any more legal or enforceable."[14]

This common law rule, that there is no property interest in the body, was adopted in the United States and has been critical in the subsequent development of the law of the body. The failure to recognize a property interest in a dead body has proven to be a significant impediment to the ability of an individual to control what happens to his or her body after death.

The recognition of something as a property interest brings with it a wide range of protections. Notably, the Constitution provides protections against the government's interference with property interests.[15] The failure to treat a person's body as a property interest therefore effectively precludes the use of a range of constitutional protections.[16] The other main value in having something designated a property interest is that when something is "property," then the law generally designates a particular person or entity as the property owner. This designation makes it much easier for claims to be asserted. As the law stands now, without a recognized property interest, much litigation occurs simply to determine which person is the appropriate decision-maker.[17]

It is perhaps due in part to this "no property in your body" rule in common law that so many states have enacted statutes that purportedly give people the ability to control what happens to their bodies after death. These statutes typically allow people to leave directions regarding the disposition of their body and/or to designate someone to make such decisions regarding its disposition.[18]

Although the statutes appear to be highly protective of people's rights to control what happens to their body after death, the reality falls short of appearances. The key reason for this is that these statutes are primarily the product of lobbying from the funeral industry, which was concerned with avoiding liability from dissenting family members. The focus of the statutes is thus to allow funeral directors to rely on instructions left by a decedent, provided they are expressed in a particular form. Although these statutes might provide some protection for people who have survivors interested in carrying out their wishes, they provide no protection where these people are missing because they have no mechanism for imposing liability for failure to fulfill the decedent's stated wishes. Moreover, many statutes that purport to grant rights of control actually limit this control in substantive ways. For example, some hold that the wishes must be carried out only if they are "reasonable and do not impose an economic or emotional hardship"[19] or if they are "reasonable under the circumstances" (taking into account such factors as the size of the estate, cultural or family customs, and the person's religious or spiritual beliefs).[20] The effect of such qualifications is that these statutes provide more of a hope than a promise that a person's wishes regarding his or her body will be carried out.

There is an additional level of uncertainty for any person interested in controlling what happens to his or her body after death: the autopsy. In a full autopsy, internal organs are removed, examined, and placed back inside the body (although not necessarily reattached). State laws generally give broad authority to conduct a full autopsy in the case of unnatural death or for any public health reason regardless of the wishes of the decedent or his or her family.[21] In addition, in many states, when conducting an autopsy, the coroner has the right to remove corneas, pituitary glands, and other organs for transplant without the consent of the decedent or his family.[22] Individuals may have personal objections to the performance of an autopsy on their body. In addition, many religious and ethnic groups (including Hmong, Orthodox Jews, Mexican Americans, Muslims, and Navajo) hold beliefs that a person enters the afterlife with the body in its condition at the time of death or that a body can feel pain for as long as several days after bodily death. Members of these groups often therefore object to autopsies as a form of proscribed "mutilation of the dead."[23] Although some states allow people to register religious objections to an autopsy, the vast majority do not. Moreover, even in states that do permit religious objections, autopsies can still be conducted if the state has an overriding need for information that can be gained from the autopsy.[24] These statutes have been widely accepted as constitutional.[25]

The other problem that emerges as a result of this lack of property interest is in determining who has decision-making authority with respect to the disposition of a body. In numerous cases the spouse and other blood relatives have disagreed over what should happen to their loved one's body. States have responded by enacting statutes—most still in force today—that list an order of preference for making this decision. The most common order starts with the husband or wife of the deceased and then goes to adult children, to parents, and finally to other blood relatives.[26] But such statutes do not resolve all the issues, and in a surprising number of cases courts are brought in to decide who has the power to control burial.[27]

Obligations toward the Body: The Right to a Christian Burial

Dead bodies must be disposed of properly or they can pose a health hazard to the living. In addition, the desire to treat dead bodies with respect is deeply engrained across different societies. American law addresses these concerns by imposing an obligation on family members to provide a proper burial for the body. One nineteenth-century treatise writer described this as the right of a deceased to a Christian burial.[28] This no doubt derived from the common law of England, where the Church of England was the official church of the state, and its court, the ecclesiastical court, had the power over the disposition of dead bodies. As these rules took root in American soil, where there was no state religion, the phrase took on a more secular meaning. This gave rise to the following explanation, as stated in an 1896 treatise on mortuary law: "The word Christian is not a denominational term, as here used, but means some proper recognition of the nature of man and the solemnity of his entrance into the world beyond. Christian burial, in this sense, is a term applicable to the Hindu, Mohammedan, and Jew as well as to the Christian. He has the right to have his remains kept secure from ill treatment, from undue exposure and from dishonor."[29]

The English commentator Sir William Blackstone, who had great influence over early American law, described the obligation of burial as the duty to bury the deceased in a manner suitable to the estate he leaves behind him. These funeral expenses were allowed to be paid before the other claims of the deceased.[30] The effect of this rule was that burial expenses could be taken care of, even if it resulted in other creditors not being paid.

The right to a proper burial figured prominently in an American case in which an elderly man who lived with his sister chose to dispose of her body "at home." As the court described it:

> In June 1938 Harriet was in failing health. She appears to have suffered some injury from a fall and during the night of June 9th she remained in a reclining chair in the front room of their home. About four o'clock in the morning of June 10th she died. The respondent [her brother] thereupon built a hot fire in the furnace in the basement of the house, tied a rope around the legs of his sister's body, dragged it down the cellar stairs, shoved it into the furnace and burned it. It was impossible to get it all into the fire box at once, but as the head and shoulders were consumed, he forced it in farther and farther until he was able to close the furnace door.[31]

The brother apparently took this course of action in compliance with his sister's expressed wishes (as well as with the intention of saving funeral expenses).[32] Nonetheless, criminal charges were brought against the elderly man. Although the court had some difficulty in determining the nature of the crime, it ultimately stated that the offense was not that the body was burned but that it was indecently burned in such a manner that, when the facts became known, the feelings and natural sentiments of the public would be outraged.[33]

The principles that inspired these rules governing the proper treatment of the body—respect for the dead and health for the living—also inspire rules against necrophilia and cannibalism.

Super Capital Punishment: Punishing the Body for Crimes of the Deceased

A critical, though largely forgotten, issue involving the historical treatment of dead bodies was the practice of desecrating the body as punishment for particularly egregious crimes.

An early example of the phenomenon occurred on 30 January 1661. On that day the bodies of the regicides Oliver Cromwell, Henry Ireton, and John Bradshaw were exhumed, dragged to London's place of execution, Tyburn, on hurdles, and hanged before a crowd of thousands. At sunset, the bodies were taken down, decapitated, and buried in a pit under Tyburn, while the heads were placed on spikes atop Westminster Hall.[34] Dismemberment of the body was understood by many as a way of punishing the traitor beyond the grave.

Although this early imposition of desecration as punishment was an ad hoc act of revenge by a returning monarch, the practice was formally established in the development of the statutory law as well. In 1752, Parliament passed "An Act for better preventing the horrid crime of murder" that required the hanging in chains or dissection of the bodies of all executed murderers so that "some further Terror and peculiar Mark of Infamy might be added to the Punishment of Death."[35] Being dismembered was viewed as an extra punishment, and murderers reputedly would try to plead guilty to another capital offense so that, although they would still be hanged, their bodies would be buried whole and not dissected.

The use of dissection as a form of super capital punishment carried over to the new United States. In 1784, for example, Massachusetts law required that a person slain in a duel would be either buried in a public place without a coffin and with a stake through his body or given to a surgeon for dissection (in case death alone was not an adequate deterrent).[36] These provisions served the dual purpose of punishing perpetrators and providing bodies for anatomical studies.

The First Wave of Change: Bodies for Anatomical Study

The basic principles regarding the law of the body were stable for many years. As society developed new uses for dead bodies, however, there was pressure to change the laws governing the control and treatment of bodies. Increased interest in anatomical study triggered the first wave.

The beginning of modern anatomical study is often attributed to the great sixteenth-century Belgian anatomist Andreas Vesalius. Vesalius dissected bodies of executed criminals and developed a set of meticulous anatomical drawings, many created by some of the leading artists of the time. Anatomical study, which we today associate exclusively with medical training, was originally made available to a much broader swath of the public. Dissection was originally a public spectacle for which people bought tickets.[37] Indeed, Vesalius's most famous book, *De humani corporis fabrica libri septem* (1543), includes an illustration of a dissection in which the open female corpse is surrounded by a veritable mob of onlookers.

In the United States, anatomical study—and the growing need for corpses—was closely linked to the formalization of medical education. Cultural historian Michael Sappol explores this link in *A Traffic of Dead Bodies.* As he explains, with the development of medicine as a profession in the eighteenth century, hands-on anatomical study became a defining feature of medical education.[38] The availability of corpses for dissection soon became an essential component of a school's success or failure. In fact, Harvard Medical School moved from Cambridge to Boston in 1810 in order to have increased access to cadavers, which, in the words of one Harvard anatomy professor, were "utterly unattainable at Cambridge."[39]

Medical education expanded rapidly in the nineteenth century: in 1800 there were just four medical schools in the United States, but by 1900 there were 160.[40] The perceived importance of anatomical study for medical students, combined with the expansion of medical schools, created a significant problem: How could schools find enough corpses for their students to dissect? Exacerbating the problem was that many Americans believed in the literal resurrection of the human body and therefore were deeply concerned that their bodies remain intact. Because the body's integrity was thought to be necessary for salvation in the afterlife, many people did not want their bodies to be subject to autopsy and research.[41] Moreover, in the nineteenth century, Americans of all classes and backgrounds were deeply concerned with having a proper burial. As Sappol writes:

> For the American bourgeoisie, the rural cemetery movement that emerged in the 1830s with its elaborately planned mausoleums, monuments, and pastoral death parks, was a means of marking off lower classes. . . . The working poor tried to assure themselves a place in funerary society by securing burials in cemeteries or churchyards that were equivalent to those of the bourgeoisie, or within bourgeois cemeteries in inferior graves and spaces. . . . [This was equally true for the poor.] If you accumulated no other capital in your life, your one bit of savings might go to pay for your burial and the burial of your loved ones, or lacking that, perhaps a shroud or a bit of stain for the plain pine box provided by the city. Such small gestures of respect worked to distinguish the poor from the absolutely indigent and friendless—and, often enough, poor whites from poorer blacks—and thereby attenuated the stigma of an impoverished death. Poor blacks, like poor whites, made every effort to avoid a pauper's death, pooling resources where possible. And the worst fate that might await an unprotected body was anatomical dissection at a medical college.[42]

Given the value of a proper burial and the widespread religious belief in a physical afterlife, it is not surprising that finding cadavers for anatomical research became an increasingly pressing problem.

Criminals became the first source of bodies. As discussed above, it was the law of England, adopted by many states in the United States, that— as a form of super capital punishment for the most heinous crimes—the bodies of executed criminals would be given to medical schools for dissection. This rule still exists in the statutes of many states, including Massachusetts, which provides that "upon conviction of murder in the first degree, the court may order the body of the convict after his execution to be dissected. The warden of the state prison shall in such case deliver it to a professor of anatomy or surgery in a medical school established by law in the commonwealth, if so requested; otherwise, he shall, unless the convict's friends desire it for interment, deliver it to any surgeon attending to receive it who will undertake to dissect it."[43]

As interest in anatomy grew, the supply of executed criminals did not keep pace with the demand (and the association of dissection with punishment hardly made it an attractive option for the public at large). Initially this gap in the market was met—as such gaps often are—by the criminal element. Grave robbery (also called "body snatching" or "resurrectionism") became a profitable enterprise, with anatomy departments paying handsomely for fresh dead bodies. At one time the going rate for a body was between ten and thirty-five dollars—this at a time when the wages of a skilled worker were between twenty and thirty dollars a *week* and a day laborer was paid a dollar a day or less.[44] Of course, if the bodies were not available, the providers sometimes needed to get creative. In several cases providers of bodies didn't wait for death: they simply killed people and then brought their bodies in for payment. In 1884 a family of three was killed in Cincinnati and sold to the Medical College of Ohio for a hundred dollars. In 1886 an elderly woman from Baltimore was murdered and sold to the University of Maryland Medical School for fifteen dollars.[45]

The most notorious of these cases occurred across the Atlantic, in Edinburgh, in 1828. William Hare (who owned a lodging house) and his friend William Burke learned how profitable the sale of bodies could be when a lodger died leaving a debt of four pounds owed to Hare. In order to recoup his losses, Burke suggested that he and Hare sell the body to Dr. Robert Knox, the most successful medical lecturer in Edinburgh. Knox offered them seven pounds, ten shillings for the body. The two were so impressed with their profit that they grew impatient waiting for their lodgers to die. They developed a system whereby they would lure people to the lodging house, get them drunk on whiskey, suffocate them, and sell their bodies to Knox. Burke and Hare were caught and put

on trial in 1829 for the murder of sixteen people (some historians estimate that they were responsible for many more deaths).[46] Although Hare
avoided punishment by becoming a witness for the king, Burke was con-
victed, receiving the fitting sentence of execution followed by dissection.
The Burke case is widely recognized as facilitating the enactment of
the Warburton Anatomy Act of 1832, which increased the availability of
corpses for dissection by providing for the transfer of unclaimed bodies
to anatomists. The Warburton Act has been credited with ending the
practice of grave robbery in Britain.[47]

In America, medical schools became both directly and indirectly involved
in the body-snatching business to meet the pressing demand for cadavers.
A letter from John Godman, one of the most distinguished anatomists
of the early nineteenth century, to John Warren, a leading anatomist at
Harvard University, provides insight to how corpses were supplied for
medical education:

> In both New York and Philadelphia, anatomists bribed public
> officials and burial-ground employees to gain unhindered access
> to the paupers buried in Potter's Field. In New York, the super-
> intending official divided the bodies into two categories. Those
> "most entitled to respect, or most likely to be called for by
> friends" were buried in Pit No. 1 and exempted from dissection;
> the rest were buried in Pit No. 2, which was plundered to sup-
> ply the medical colleges. In Philadelphia, however, the anato-
> mists were entitled to "all the subjects buried in the two public
> grounds." If schools or physicians differed over who should get
> an allotment of bodies, the dispute was to be settled by the mayor
> —a high reaching conspiracy that resulted in a harvest of about
> 450 bodies per school year.[48]

Although grave robbery was sometimes left to the "professionals," it
was also a rite of passage that many medical students undertook themselves. William James McKnight—a doctor who later became a state
senator in Pennsylvania—published a number of articles describing his
grave-robbing experiences in medical school. As he explained in one description:

On the day of Southerland's death Simons [a local doctor] organized a "Resurrection party." Young McKnight was one of the
five doctors invited to join the forthcoming nocturnal mission.
From his old preceptor he received permission to use an empty
house for the proposed demonstration. Shortly before midnight
on 31 October 1857 the party, with several of its members "filled
to the brim with Monongahela whiskey," set out for the cemetery. They were armed with a mattock [a tool similar to a pickax],
a shovel, and a quantity of rope. Upon reaching the cemetery,
McKnight and another member of the party, which had now increased to seven, were assigned as watchers. The others were to
"lift" the body. Once the stimulating effect of whiskey had worn
off, several of the latter lost their zeal. Nevertheless the coffin was
finally uncovered, broken open, and the corpse withdrawn by
means of a rope that had been passed around it. After the burial
vestments were stuffed into the coffin, the grave was carefully restored, and the naked body placed on a bier and carried to its
appointed place.[49]

Grave robbery by medical students was deeply disturbing to the public
and gave rise to mass opposition. In the hundred years between 1785 and
1885, Americans expressed their anger at the anatomists in at least seventeen riots. These riots affected nearly every institution of medical learn-
ing. At Columbia University, one riot went on for two days and seven
people were killed.[50]

Moreover, the body-snatching epidemic prompted a crisis in the legal system, which had adopted the principle of nullius in bonis. Because the dead person belonged to nobody, no one had the legal authority to complain when a body was stolen. Early cases focused on the theft
of the clothes that the body wore, but this was only a misdemeanor and
couldn't provide punishment commensurate with the pain of loved ones
at the theft of a body. One response to this was the widespread enactment of legislation prohibiting the desecration of graves and the stealing
of corpses.[51] Because the underlying need for corpses persisted, however,
this criminalization did little to stop the activity.

The practice of grave robbery continued until the passage of new legislation known as anatomy acts. These laws provided a legal venue for medical schools to do that which they were already doing illegally—taking the bodies of the poor and dispossessed, whose burial costs would otherwise have been borne by the state.[52] Anatomy laws were pitched to legislators as providing a double benefit: they would save local jurisdictions the cost of burying the indigent while providing a stream of cadavers to medical schools. Proponents of anatomy acts also argued that passage of these acts would discourage people from becoming wards of the state. Most important for the middle and upper classes, if medical schools had a legal source of bodies, the risk that corpses of the affluent would be stolen would greatly diminish.

Massachusetts passed the first anatomy act in the United States in 1831. This statute, "An Act . . . to protect the Sepulchers of the Dead," was carefully crafted to limit controversy. Its purported goal—-trumpeted in its name—was to prevent grave robbery. And to avoid charges that it was targeted at poor people, the law used the term "unclaimed" rather than "indigent" bodies. Although in theory, a wealthy person could die and his or her body could remain "unclaimed," to protect against this happening, the law provided exemptions for "travelers" as well as a waiting period for other bodies to be claimed. It also limited its application to those living in Boston and provided an exception for poor people who had been long-time residents (called "town paupers.") After applying all of these rules, the anatomy act (as well as others that followed) most commonly applied to the growing population of German, Irish, Italian, and Jewish immigrants that had settled in the state's urban areas.[53]

Anatomy acts were enacted in several other states, including Connecticut (1833), New Hampshire (1834), Michigan (1844), New York (1854), and Pennsylvania (1867, and amended in 1881), but they remained a source of controversy, and the majority were repealed shortly after enactment. By the end of the Civil War, only the Massachusetts and New York anatomy statutes remained in effect.[54]

In the postbellum era, medical science began to produce significant advances that produced dividends for the American people and softened popular sentiment toward the medical profession. Along with this shift in sentiment followed an acceptance of the necessity of anatomy acts. By the turn of the twentieth century, many states had anatomy acts, and Congress passed an anatomy act for the District of Columbia.

Today many medical schools meet their need for cadavers through people's voluntary donation of their bodies. This is particularly true for the most prestigious institutions, some of which have a surplus of cadavers and thus have stringent requirements for donation.[55] Less well known institutions, however, often struggle to meet their demand for bodies, and anatomy acts continue to play a role in meeting that demand.[56] Today's anatomy acts still apply to "unclaimed bodies." Rather than being directed to residents of poor houses, however, they are more likely to apply to people in prisons and hospitals who would otherwise be buried or cremated at government expense. The statutes continue to provide protections against more affluent people being unwittingly caught by retaining an exception for travelers and providing waiting periods. In addition, modern anatomy statutes have added exceptions for those who have served in the military. However, those who do not meet these exceptions generally give up their rights to control what happens to their bodies after death; few states allow people to opt out of these provisions.

The Second Wave of Change: Bodies for Organ Transplants

Just as societal changes brought about more demand for dead bodies, scientific and technological developments also changed the landscape. Early in December 1967, a young South African surgeon took the healthy heart of a young woman who had been killed in an automobile accident and transplanted it to the body of a man dying of heart disease. The surgeon, Dr. Christiaan Barnard, later said that he knew that the transplant was a surgical success when he applied electrodes and the heart resumed beating. Although the transplant recipient died eighteen days later of pneumonia, this operation was a milestone in a new field of life-extending surgery that dramatically increased awareness of the potential value of human cadavers and transformed legal issues involving the dead in fundamental ways. As one scholar has described it: "Organ transplantation radically changed the nature of the problem by bringing into the picture for the first time the highest principle of law, medicine, ethics and religion: saving human life. This principle was not previously relevant in the disposition of corpses."[57]

Over the next twenty years, with the development of new antirejection treatments, organ transplants offered promises of treatment to more and more people. Yet for these promises to be fulfilled, the legal regimen needed to be transformed. The greatest difficulty facing the field was in providing organs for the rapidly increasing number of people who could benefit from transplants.[58] To address this problem, legislators enacted a series of laws to encourage the donation of organs. These laws had to provide new rules for controlling the disposition of cadavers, but they also needed to alter the rules regarding the very definition of death itself.

The first problem was that it was not clear who had the power to donate a human body to provide the organs for transplant. American law had developed based on the common law legal principle that a corpse belongs to no one. (Thus, just as Henry Crookenden was not allowed to give his body to his friend Eliza Williams for her to cremate it, there was no clear way for an individual to donate his or her body to a medical institution for the purpose of providing organs.) The rule may have been adequate at a time when a body was primarily an obligation, something to be handled and disposed of, but it became deeply problematic as the potential value of—and thereby the number of people interested in—dead bodies increased.

To address this dilemma, shortly after the famous heart transplant a group of influential lawyers, judges, and professors got together to draft model legislation specifically addressed to the issue of cadaver organ donation. This model statute, the Uniform Anatomical Gift Act (UAGA), provided a mechanism for the donation of bodies at death for transplant and was highly successful: within five years of its proposal in 1968, it was adopted by all fifty states and the District of Columbia.

The UAGA accomplished several goals. Most important, it provided a clear mechanism for people to donate their organs at death. Prior law had been a mishmash of rules that considered a variety of factors in determining who could make decisions regarding a person's body after death. Under the UAGA, individuals could state their wishes to donate their body either through a provision in their will or by a witnessed document

(usually in the form of an organ donor card issued by a state's department of motor vehicles). The UAGA also provided a mechanism through
which family members (in ranked order) could donate part or all of
the decedent's body. By creating a statute that was adopted throughout
the United States, the UAGA also provided national uniformity for the
laws governing organ donation. This increased the ability of organ donor
programs to find compatible matches between donors and recipients
throughout the country. Finally, the UAGA established standards under
which organs could be donated and under which organizations could receive organ donations.[59]

The UAGA was extremely successful in providing mechanisms for donation and national uniformity. However, it was less successful in procur-
ing enough donors to meet the burgeoning demand of potential transplant recipients. As one commentator put it almost twenty years later:

> An overriding problem common to all organ transplantation pro-
> grams as well as to the well-established programs in tissue bank-
> ing (for corneal, skin and bone transplantation) is the serious
> gap between the need for the organs and tissues and the supply
> of donors. Despite substantial support for transplantation and a
> general willingness to donate organs and tissues after death, the
> demand far exceeds the supply. At any one time, there are an esti-
> mated 8,000 to 10,000 people waiting for a donor organ to be-
> come available.[60]

In response to the problem of insufficient organ donations, states incor-
porated two types of provisions into their statutes: "required request"
and "presumed consent." These provisions sought to increase the number of available organs while taking into account the individual's desire to
control what happens to his or her body or the body of a loved one.
However, the balance was struck very differently in the two provisions.

Required request provisions sought to encourage more people to think
about organ donation by requiring hospitals to ask individuals about organ donation on admission to the hospital and to ask family members for
permission to retrieve organs from patients who died.[61] States generally
accepted these provisions, and they remain in force.[62] In addition, the
federal government put its imprimatur on the required request approach

by mandating it for hospitals that receive Medicare and Medicaid reimbursement.[63]

Presumed consent provisions also have as their goal the procurement of more organs for donation. Under presumed consent statutes, however, the focus is more directly on society's needs for organs and less on preserving individual or family control. Presumed consent statutes seek to increase the number of organs available for transplant by presumptively eliminating the need for consent in certain situations. These statutes provide that in any case in which a body is subject to autopsy, the coroner is entitled to donate parts of the decedent's body for transplant purposes, unless the coroner has direct knowledge of a refusal or contrary indication by the decedent or the decedent's family.[64] This last provision might seem to protect the decedent or his or her family in that their objections must be taken into account. However, because the coroner is under no obligation to inquire about the preference of the deceased or the decedent's family members and is relieved of liability as long as he or she does not know of any contrary instructions, this arrangement encourages coroners to embrace ignorance rather than to search for true intent.

Presumed consent statutes apply only to cases in which the body is under investigation by a state medical examiner. (These autopsies should not be confused with private autopsies requested by family members.) Bodies are typically subject to investigation by state coroners in cases of homicide or suspicious death. Who is most likely to be subject to these mandatory autopsies? Most commonly it has been young, male black and Latino victims of gang violence or drug overdose. As Michelle Goodwin points out in her book *Black Markets,* "During this period of violence in the 1980's and into the 1990's came rising death tolls of young Blacks and Latinos and the promulgation of presumed consent laws. These two overlapping occurrences were a tragic coincidence."[65]

The *Los Angeles Times* put a human face on this phenomenon when it investigated the case of Carlos Guidina, a young victim of urban violence who was shot and killed in Los Angeles in 1997. Although family members had specifically told the coroner's office that they did not want any organs donated, their objection came too late. Without telling the family, the corneas of the young man had already been harvested and delivered to the local eye bank on the coroner's authorization. It turns out that the eye bank and the coroner's office had a mutually beneficial arrangement in which the coroner's office was paid about $250 on average for a set of corneas, which the eye bank then sold to transplant institutions for a "processing fee" of $3,400. Over five years, the coroner's office had received more than a million dollars from the sale of corneas, while the eye bank undoubtedly had profits many times greater. The only people who made no profit on this transaction were the decedents (more than 80 percent of them people of color) and their families. Indeed, had they made any money they would have been surprised, because in the vast majority of cases, people had no idea that their loved one's body parts had been harvested. As Goodwin points out, the presumed consent laws operate in a culture of silence. In one survey, more than 90 percent of survey participants in a state with presumed consent laws were unaware that such a law existed.[66]

Presumed consent statutes have been subject to court scrutiny because several families have complained about the removal of corneal tissue for donation to eye banks without their consent.[67] These statutes have generally been upheld on the theory that first, neither the decedent nor a family member has a property interest in the decedent's body, and second, whatever constitutional right of privacy may exist with respect to the integrity of the body, such right is personal and ends with death.[68] The one case that ruled in favor of the family, *Brotherton v. Cleveland*, failed to find a property right in the decedent's body but nonetheless held that the decedent's wife had a legitimate claim of entitlement protected under federal law.[69]

Many other countries have presumed consent statutes.[70] However, these statutes differ from United States law in two important ways: these statutes provide mechanisms through which people can opt-out of presumed consent and know that their wishes will be upheld, and these statutes apply to all individuals—not just those whose deaths are subject to state investigation.

Just as some people's bodies are being used for organ transplants without their consent or the consent of their families, another group of people has expressed interest in becoming organ donors but has been unable to do so: death row inmates. Jonathan Nobles was sentenced to death in Texas for the murder of two young women. While in prison, Nobles underwent a religious conversion and sought to donate his organs so that he could do something positive after "bringing so much darkness into this world."[71] The Texas Department of Criminal Justice denied his request.

Death row inmates cannot donate their organs primarily because of the methods of execution used in the United States. Five methods of execution are in use: electrocution, lethal injection, gas chamber, hanging, and firing squad. Although each method is different, they share one important feature: each prevents effective organ procurement because the organs are either destroyed or rendered useless during the time that elapses between the administration of the execution and the pronouncement of death.[72] This means that people executed for crimes cannot donate their organs for transplant.

Some states have attempted to adopt legislation that would make it easier for inmates to donate their organs. In 2000 a representative from the Florida legislature proposed a bill to allow death row inmates to donate their organs on execution if the organs were still useable. There was strong opposition to this bill from organ procurement organizations, and many were concerned about the ethical, scientific, and legal issues. This opposition kept the bill from becoming law. In Missouri a "Life for a Life" bill was proposed that would allow an inmate to donate a kidney in exchange for a commuted sentence. This bill failed owing to ethical concerns over offering such an incentive.[73]

One proposed Arizona law even suggested that inmates should be given the choice of death by lethal injection or by organ removal. Apparently, death can be accomplished painlessly and quickly by the mere process of organ removal under anesthesia. This method of execution produces no harmful effects on the organs. It would, however, create an ethical dilemma for physicians, who would be violating both the Hippocratic Oath and the American Medical Association's prohibition against physicians' participating in executions.[74]

Much complexity underlies the decision whether to allow executed criminals to donate their organs, including issues of whether prisoners have truly consented to have their organs donated and perceived opportunities for abuse. In China, for example, prisoners are routinely executed and their organs are reputedly sold by the government at large profit.[75]

Another concern is undoubtedly at play here, however: the opportunity to donate organs is an opportunity to leave a positive mark on the world, and there is a widely held belief that people who have committed the most heinous crimes should not be allowed an opportunity to leave such a legacy. The mother of one of Jonathan Nobles's victims said that Nobles lost his rights, including the right to donate organs, when he murdered her daughter.[76]

Redefining Death

The most significant, and in some ways stunning, change of law that was required by the development of the ability to transplant organs was the very definition of death itself.

The legal and moral duties owed to living persons differ significantly from those owed to dead persons. The distinction between the living and the dead is thus a critical one. Yet the question of when death occurs is surprisingly more complicated than one might imagine. This problem has both practical and theoretical dimensions.

The challenge of determining when death occurred was historically a practical concern. People knew (or at least thought they knew) what death was; they just didn't have the tools to determine whether death had in fact occurred. The problem of premature burial was thus very real. One compilation from the seventeenth century reveals 219 instances of narrow escape from premature burial, 149 cases of actual premature burial, ten cases in which bodies were accidentally dissected before death, and two cases in which embalming was started on the not-yet-dead.[77]

The risks of premature burial continued through the nineteenth century and into the early twentieth century. Edgar Allan Poe captured these fears in some of his most famous short stories, including "The Premature Burial" and "The Cask of Amontillado."

The fear of premature burial prompted people to invent ingenious solutions. In 1868 a New Jersey man was granted a patent for his design of a coffin outfitted with a tube that contained a bell and a ladder, enabling the entombed individual to climb to safety or summon others for help.[78] Another response was the development of the waiting mortuary. This was a holding place where the presumed dead could be kept before burial, giving them a last opportunity to show that they had life in them before being buried. Some mortuaries placed a bell on the deceased's foot. If the person moved, the bell would ring, notifying the attendant that the individual was still alive. (Some attribute the phrase "saved by the bell" to the waiting mortuary for this reason.)

There was also more organized response to this fear as well. The Association for Prevention of Premature Burial was formed in London in 1899, and a year later its American counterpart, the Society for the Prevention of Premature Burial, was established. These organizations sought the enactment of laws to bring professional medical personnel into the determination of whether death had occurred. We see the results of their work today in statutes that require death certificates to be issued with the signature of a licensed physician who can attest to the fact of the person's death.

The practical problem of discerning whether the signs of death had occurred largely abated in the twentieth century with the development of medical technology that gave the physician more accurate ways of measuring heart and brain activity. Though the practical issues were solved, a more significant problem remained: the theoretical definition of death. This issue is not as clear-cut as one might think. Although people conceive of death as occurring in a moment (and the legal world requires this as well), in biological terms, death is not a discrete event but a gradual process.[79] Thus, even after a person's heart stops beating, other muscle, skin, and bone cells may live on for several days. Picking a moment in this process and calling that the moment of death is in some ways arbitrary and has had a complicated history.

The debate about what constitutes death began in earnest in 1740 with the writings of the physician and anatomist Jean-Jacques Winslow. Winslow was terrified by the thought of premature burial and sought—unsuccessfully—to discover a definitive surgical test to determine whether death had occurred (considering but ultimately rejecting such tests as pinpricks and incisions). Winslow came by his fear honestly. As a child he had twice been abandoned for dead, only to revive and discover that he had been placed in a coffin.[80]

Building on the work of Winslow, some argued that all signs of death, except for putrefaction (decomposition of the body), were inconclusive and therefore that a corpse should be dissected, embalmed, or buried only after it had begun to decompose, because "the laws of Religion and of humanity forbid advancing death even one moment."[81]

As much as using putrefaction of the body as a standard for death protected people against premature burial, however, it created significant problems of its own. First of all, at a time when most people died at home, waiting for a body to decay was not simply an inconvenience but a health risk to the family and neighbors of the deceased. Second, the putrefaction standard also posed a problem for anatomists (a growing group in the eighteenth and nineteenth centuries), who needed to study cadavers before they had been changed by decay.[82]

Fortunately for neighbors and anatomists, medical tools were developed that enabled medical professionals to adopt a new standard for death: the cessation of the beating heart and the breathing of the lungs. These "cardiopulmonary criteria" were widely adopted by the medical profession and in turn allowed the definition of death to be viewed as a technical problem that could be solved by the application of medical expertise.[83] This resulted in the development of the almost universal law that "a person is dead when a physician says so."[84]

For a brief period, then, there seemed to be some certainty in the situation—an agreed upon standard (cessation of heart and lung function) and a mode of determining whether the standard had occurred—but such certainty would not last. The continuing development of medical technology raised new issues regarding the appropriateness of the cardiopulmonary standard of death.

The first of these was the development in the mid-twentieth century of the mechanical ventilator, which made it possible to support a person's heart and lung function even after brain function had ceased. A person's heartbeat could now continue even when the patient had no discernible brain activity and respiration was mechanically sustained. This put hospitals in the difficult position of maintaining care for individuals who seemed to be more dead than alive.[85] It also raised an additional problem that under a cardiopulmonary definition of death, the removal of a mechanical ventilator from a person with no brain activity technically constituted murder. This resulted in some peculiar legal cases, including one case in the 1970s in which a defendant charged with murder argued that the doctors who removed the life support, and not he, caused the death of the victim.[86]

The ability to transplant organs raised another problem with using the cardiopulmonary definition of death. After the heart stops pumping, organs quickly begin to decay and soon are no longer suitable for transplant. The cardiopulmonary definition of death thus impeded the availability of organs for transplant.

In 1968 a highly influential report issued by an ad hoc committee at Harvard Medical School came to the rescue by proposing a new definition of death: cessation of brain function. This definition made a certain degree of sense in a society that associates personal identity with the brain. Happily, it also served the goals of organ transplants by providing that organs could be harvested from a body after the brain had ceased functioning, even if the person was still breathing and still had a heart rate (due to mechanical ventilation). Shortly after this report appeared, all fifty states had adopted some version of the brain death standard either by statute or case law.

The most widely adopted statute, the Uniform Definition of Death Act, provides that a person can be declared dead when he or she has sustained either irreversible cessation of circulatory and respiratory functions or irreversible cessation of all functions of the entire brain.[87] This statute has been adopted in forty-three states. States that have not adopted the Uniform Definition of Death Act have either adopted their own statutes or developed case law that allows the use of brain death as a standard for death. Brain death has also been adopted as a standard throughout much of the rest of the world.

One of the last countries to adopt the brain death standard was Japan, which until 2009 maintained the cardiopulmonary standard for death. Much has been written to explain Japan's outlier status on this issue, but one factor that seems relevant is the differing view in Japan of what it means to be a person. In the West, personhood is often equated with an individual's brain or consciousness (building on René Descartes's famous statement, "I think therefore I am"). However, under the Japanese view, the "person" is not equated with individual consciousness, nor is the person located in the brain. Rather, personhood is diffused throughout the mind and body and is a condition that is fundamentally social rather than individualistic.[88]

In order to provide organs for transplant, Japan's Organ Transplantation Law, enacted in 1997, allowed brain death to be used as a standard provided that the person had recorded his or her preference on a donor card and that the family also consented. Although this law was a significant departure from the traditional Japanese notion of death, Japan still had the strictest standards in the world regarding the conditions for becoming an organ donor, and the statute did little to ease the Japanese organ shortage crisis. In the twelve years after its enactment, only eighty-one cases of organs being donated from brain-dead patients were reported. The organ donation problem was particularly serious for infants and young children since children under the age of fifteen could not create valid organ donation cards. This made organ transplants for children practically impossible owing to the differences in organ sizes. As a result of the scarcity of organs available for transplantation, many Japanese citizens traveled abroad to receive organs, a state of affairs that resulted in much criticism of the 1997 Japanese law.[89]

In response to concerns about the scarcity of organs for children as well as apprehension that the World Health Organization would enact guidelines that would prevent people from going overseas for transplants, Japan changed its law in 2009 to allow organs to be harvested from brain-dead patients, even in the absence of a valid donor card, provided that the person had never opposed organ donation while alive and that family members gave their consent.[90]

Despite this near-universal adoption of the brain death standard, this is not likely to be the end of the matter. There are several reasons. First, a person who is brain-dead does not necessarily appear dead to outsiders. To many people, it is disconcerting to call a person who is warm and has a heartbeat "dead." Moreover, many religions have their own official views of when death occurs, and these standards are sometimes at odds with the brain death standard. Finally, as technology develops, it is able to detect increasingly subtle levels of brain activity, calling into doubt the ability to measure brain death with any accuracy.

As a result of these issues, disagreements can arise regarding whether a person is in fact dead. This conflict played out in a 2007 case involving Cho Fook Cheng, a seventy-two-year-old grandfather who suffered a heart attack the day after Thanksgiving. He was brought to the hospital and placed on a ventilator. Soon thereafter, the doctors declared Cheng dead based on the brain death standard and sought to have him removed from life support. The family, however, practiced a Taiwanese form of Buddhism in which a person is not considered dead until the heart stops beating. The case was heading for a court showdown but was rendered moot when Cheng's heart stopped on its own.[91] Yet, based on the plain meaning of the governing statutes, as well as case law from other jurisdictions, it seems likely that the hospital would have been within its legal rights to remove life support. Once a person is declared dead under the governing authority, the family is not entitled to demand life-support measures.[92]

In response to such difficulties, some scholars have suggested that the moment of death be at least partially a function of individual choice. New Jersey has enacted a statute that allows a patient's religious belief to be taken into account in determining whether death has occurred. New Jersey's law is similar to the law of other jurisdictions in providing for doctors to apply either the cardiopulmonary or brain death standard, but it goes on to provide that the brain death standard is not to be used if the physician authorized to declare death has reason to believe that the brain death standard would violate the person's religious beliefs. In such a case, only the cardiopulmonary standard is to be used.[93]

Other states may follow the New Jersey model, particularly if courts accept the argument put forth by at least one legal scholar that the ability to choose one's definition of death is mandated by the Constitution's protection of the free exercise of religion.[94]

The Next Wave: Posthumous Conception, Cryonics, and Beyond

One way that people think of themselves as living on after death is through their children. In the vast majority of cases procreation occurs solely among the living. However, medical technology has now advanced to such a state that things once firmly in the realm of science fiction—

such as reproducing after death—have become commonplace. There is, moreover, no end in sight for scientific developments, and one can easily imagine a time in the not-too-distant future when human cloning and cryonics become viable. Just as the growth of anatomical studies and the development of organ transplant technology put pressure on prior legal structures, these most recent developments pose many unresolved challenges to our legal system.

Posthumous Reproduction and Conception

Although traditional procreative activities are limited to the living, there are now many ways in which a person can be involved in the conception or carrying of a child after death.

Historically, the only situation in which a person could posthumously parent a child was when a man impregnated a woman and then died before the baby was born. Under English common law as well as current law in the United States, a child who was conceived during the father's life but born after the father's death would be treated as if born during the father's life. The only issue was in making the determination that the child was truly the child of the deceased husband. Under the common law of England, inheritance rights were limited to children born of a lawful marriage, so this determination was made by doing a physical examination of the man's wife. If the baby was, in the words of the common law, "en ventre sa mere" (in the womb of the mother), then the child would be considered the child of the dead husband.

This rule regarding posthumous children was limited to the situation where a child was born to a married woman whose husband died while she was pregnant. The reason for this limitation was the English common law rule that a child born of unmarried parents was "filius nullis," the child of no one, and could not inherit from either the father or the mother. The United States no longer follows the rule requiring parents to be married, and the parent-child relationship extends to every parent and child regardless of the parents' marital status. This expands the scope of cases in which paternity can be established.

Physical examination of the mother is no longer necessary to establish paternity because it can now be determined through DNA testing. A key remaining issue, however, is whether testing is available for the person who wishes to prove paternity. Some states require that paternity be established during the father's life, but others allow it to be established at any time. In those states that allow paternity to be established after the death of the father, there are cases in which courts have authorized exhuming a body for purposes of determining paternity.[95] Some states have limited posthumous DNA testing to less invasive methods (such as testing stored samples retained by the coroner from the autopsy). As DNA testing has become more accurate, however, the trend has been to allow posthumous DNA testing even when the testing requires exhuming the body.[96]

It was previously extremely rare for a child to be born after one or both of the parents' death. Modern medical technologies have made this much more common. A variety of modes of posthumous conception flourish today, including such possibilities as embryos created and frozen before death being implanted after death; genetic material being exhumed from dead bodies and preserved for use in posthumous conception; and pregnant women becoming brain-dead before the birth of their child but continuing to carry the fetus to term. Each of these cases raises complex legal questions.

Frozen Embryos and Gametes

Although posthumous reproduction was previously possible only when embryos were implanted in the mother's womb before the father's death (en ventre sa mere), it has now become possible—indeed relatively common—to freeze embryos and other reproductive matter for later use, leaving them "en ventre sa frigidaire," as it is termed.[97] These embryos and gametes can be defrosted later for gestation, even after the death of one or both of the biological parents.

Reproductive material is stored during a person's life under a variety of circumstances:

• *Embryos.* Couples undergoing fertility treatment often create multiple embryos that are frozen for future use. It is estimated that there are approximately four hundred thousand frozen embryos in storage facilities in the United States. These embryos can be safely stored for fifty years or more and can be implanted in either the genetic mother or a surrogate.[98]

- *Sperm.* There are many situations in which a man's fertility can be impaired. To maintain opportunities for reproduction, cancer patients, astronauts, athletes vulnerable to groin injuries, and soldiers going off to war often freeze their sperm for later use in the event that their fertility is compromised.[99] It is believed that sperm can be safely frozen for an unlimited time. This sperm can later be implanted in the donor's wife or girlfriend or in a surrogate.

- *Eggs.* Like men, women also face situations that may impair their fertility (such as treatment for cancer or exposure to hazardous materials) and may seek to preserve their chance to bear children in the future. Owing to the delicate cellular structure of eggs, it is very difficult to freeze them for later use. The preferred mode of preserving fertility for a woman is therefore to have eggs extracted and then to create embryos with a known or anonymous sperm donor for later implantation. If the woman dies, the embryo could be carried by a surrogate.

These cases raise significant legal issues involving who determines the use of frozen reproductive material after the death of the donor and when a person will be treated as the parent of a posthumously conceived child, particularly for purposes of inheritance and other survivor benefits.

Who determines the use of frozen embryos or gametes? In the United States this issue has been left entirely in the private realm, to be worked out by contracts between donors and clinics and then, in the event of disputes, through tort and contract litigation.[100] There is no comprehensive federal or state statutory system governing the disposition or regulation of embryos and other reproductive matter.[101] This is unlike other countries in which laws directly address this issue. For example, Italy has outlawed posthumous births, and in the United Kingdom, the Human Fertilisation and Embryology Authority regulates fertility clinics and the types of agreements into which they can enter.

The use of reproductive material has generally been left in the control of donors. Thus, standard agreements of sperm banks and fertility clinics include provisions that allow donors to direct disposition of embryos and other reproductive matter in the event of the donor's death. Although there have been cases where family members of a deceased sperm donor have argued against using the sperm in posthumous reproduction on public policy grounds, these arguments have generally been rejected and the agreements have been upheld.

The leading case in this area is *Hecht v. Superior Court* (1993).[102] In that case, William Kane had deposited fifteen vials of sperm in a California sperm bank. In a number of documents, including the donation form signed at the sperm bank, a provision in his will, and a letter to his adult children, Kane expressed his wish that the sperm be used by his live-in girlfriend, Deborah Hecht, for artificial insemination either before or after Kane's death. Kane was deeply troubled. Shortly after he deposited his sperm, Kane flew to Las Vegas and committed suicide.

Kane's two adult children from a prior marriage sought to prevent Hecht from using Kane's sperm for posthumous reproduction. At trial, they argued that it was against public policy to allow the birth of a child who would never know his father and that it would disrupt Kane's existing family by creating after-born children. (Kane's children appeared to have larger complaints against Hecht as well. In court papers they alleged that Hecht was aware of Kane's "disturbed plan" to end his life—having helped him purchase a one-way ticket and driven him to the airport—and that she had convinced Kane to allow her to have his child after his death and to leave her a substantial amount of his property to raise and care for this child.)[103] The trial court agreed with Kane's adult children and ordered the sperm destroyed. On appeal, however, the California Court of Appeal held that Hecht's use of the sperm for posthumous reproduction was not against public policy and should be allowed.

What if there is no written agreement addressing what happens to the reproductive material in the event of death? Should reproductive material be treated like other property and pass by intestacy or by the terms of a decedent's will? Again, there is little law directly governing this question (perhaps in part because sperm banks address this issue in their storage agreements), although the existing case law suggests that courts are unlikely to treat reproductive matter in the same manner as other property. As the *Kane* court stated: "A man's sperm or a woman's ova or a couple's embryos are not the same as a quarter of land, a cache of cash, or a favorite limousine. Rules appropriate to the disposition of the latter are not necessarily appropriate for the former."[104]

Based on this view that sperm is a special kind of property, the California Court of Appeal in a later case ruled that regardless of any property settlement entered into by Kane and Hecht's children (they had agreed to an eighty-twenty division of property), the sperm could *only* be used as intended by Kane. Even if others received the sperm as part of a general property settlement, they could not use it in any way other than in accordance with Kane's wishes because to do so would "violate not only the decedent's intent, but also his most 'fundamental right' to choose the genetic inheritance he leaves on this earth."[105]

The rules that have been adopted in the United States giving donors control over the disposition of their frozen reproductive matter have had the effect of increasing the number of posthumous pregnancies and births, resulting in a large number of children who have been conceived after the death of one or both of their parents. This gives rise to the question of whether a child conceived after a parent's death will be treated as the child of the deceased parent.

Whether a person is treated as another person's child has both emotional and legal significance. From a legal perspective, this determination can have implications for a variety of issues, including:

- Whether the child can inherit from the deceased parent;
- Whether the child can inherit from other relatives of the deceased parent;
- Whether the relatives of the deceased parent can inherit from the child;
- Whether the child can claim Social Security benefits as the child of the deceased parent;
- Whether the deceased parent's estate can be held liable for the support of the child; and,
- Whether the child can sue for wrongful death of the deceased parent.[106]

Although this issue has been the subject of much scholarly writing and some model legislation, there has been far less development in enacted legislation and case law.

There is a continuum of options for the law in addressing this situation. At one end of the spectrum, the law could have a "bright-line test" (a clearly defined rule or standard) requiring conception before a person's death in order for the deceased person to be treated as the parent of any resulting child. The advantage of this position is that at the time of a person's death, the individual can be certain that his or her legal status as a parent has been fixed. This reasoning has been adopted by two state courts in denying petitions to treat posthumously conceived children as children of the predeceased father for purposes of Social Security benefits.[107] This is also the position of the Uniform Status of Children of Assisted Conception Act, promulgated in 1988.[108] Only two jurisdictions, North Dakota and Virginia, have adopted this statute. Because the issues this legislation considered have since been addressed in the 2002 Uniform Parentage Act (UPA), other jurisdictions are unlikely to enact this model statute.

At the other end of the spectrum, the law could have a bright-line test that provides that posthumously conceived children always be treated as the child of the genetic parent for inheritance and other purposes, regardless of when they are conceived. This position arguably provides the greatest protection for posthumously conceived children. However, it raises serious practical problems, particularly in its application to the rules of inheritance, since a person's estate cannot be distributed until all possible heirs are identified. Because genetic material can be used many years after being stored, this rule would essentially make it impossible to close an estate for so long as there was stored genetic material. Mindful of this problem, no court or legislature has adopted this rule.

The few courts that have allowed posthumously conceived children to be treated as the child of the predeceased parent have chosen a middle ground, providing that a posthumously conceived child will be treated as the child of a deceased genetic parent if, first, the parent intended for his or her genetic material to be used for posthumous reproduction and, second, the child is born within a reasonable time after the parent's death.[109] This is similar to the position adopted in the 2002 Uniform Parentage Act. This model statute, adopted in seven states, provides a general rule that posthumously conceived children are not treated as children of the deceased parent (similar to the rule provided in the Uniform Status of

Children of Assisted Conception Act). Rather than having a bright-line test, however, it also provides an exception for cases where the deceased spouse consented in a record that if assisted reproduction were to occur after death, the deceased individual would be a parent of the child.[110]

Exhuming Reproductive Material from the Dead

Most posthumous conceptions use frozen embryos and other reproductive matter. In these cases, the donor, by virtue of having stored gametes or embryos during life, has demonstrated a desire and willingness to have his or her genetic material used to create a child. Recently, however, there has been a new mode of posthumous reproduction that does not involve any level of buy-in by the gamete provider: retrieving sperm from men who are recently deceased, brain-dead, comatose, or in a persistent vegetative state for use in posthumous procreation. The first report of a successful posthumous sperm retrieval occurred in 1980. Although there is little data about how often posthumous sperm retrieval occurs, it is clear that these requests are increasingly being made and granted.[111] And although this issue has not yet come up for women —because it is not currently technologically feasible to harvest viable eggs from dead women—it is likely a matter of time before such a procedure is available.[112]

Who decides whether this posthumous retrieval of reproductive material will occur? In the United States, there is no statutory or case law addressing this issue. Instead, these decisions are being made by emergency room doctors and urologists responding to requests of grieving family members (sometimes, but not always, with the advice of in-house hospital attorneys and hospital protocols).

In the absence of law, a number of hospitals and the American Society for Reproductive Medicine have issued guidelines for when posthumous gamete retrieval should occur. All of these proposals start with the notion that some form of premortem consent should be required, but the difference is whether explicit consent is required or whether there will be a presumption of consent in the absence of evidence to the contrary.[113] In most cases, posthumous sperm retrieval will occur in cases where there is little evidence as to what the decedent intended, so the presumptions will dictate the outcome.

Should children born from exhumed sperm be treated as the children of the deceased parent? The posthumous conception cases have all required some degree of consent by the decedent parent. Based on these standards, children conceived as a result of posthumous gamete retrieval could not be eligible to be treated as the children of the deceased parent. If these procedures become more common, however, courts will need to address the equity of preventing children conceived from posthumously exhumed sperm from establishing a legal connection (including possible inheritance rights) from their biological fathers.

Brain-Dead Mother

As discussed above, the definition of death has changed in recent years from the heart standard (cessation of pulmonary and circulatory function) to the brain standard (irreversible cessation of brain function). This new standard has enabled something else to occur that was never before possible: a dead woman having the capacity to continue to carry a child through gestation.

There are numerous recorded cases in which a brain-dead woman has been kept on artificial life support so that she could carry a baby to term.[114] Although some cases have been for relatively short periods, there have been cases where a brain-dead woman has been kept on life support for more than three months to increase the chance of survival for the unborn child.[115] In such cases, the law is clear that the mother will be treated as the mother of any child subsequently born to her because she is both the provider of the genetic material and the carrier of the child. But these cases raise a more complicated question: Who should determine whether the mother will be removed from life support (as would ordinarily happen in the case of brain death) or kept on life support until the baby is ready to be born?

End-of-life decisions are ordinarily governed by the legal principle that each person has a constitutionally protected right to refuse medical treatment and that the individual's wishes, as expressed in an advance directive or through a health-care proxy, should be respected.[116] However, the majority of American states provide by statute that if a woman is pregnant, her advance directive regarding end-of-life care is to be disregarded.[117] Moreover, because the mother is now technically "dead," it is not at all clear that the end-of-life directive continues to apply.

There is limited case law on this issue. One case from Georgia, however, shows just how thorny such legal issues can be. Donna Piazzi was unconscious when she was brought to the hospital. Her condition deteriorated to the point where she was declared dead (based on the brain death standard). The husband and family of the woman sought to have her removed from life support so that the body could be buried. The hospital, however, objected on the basis that Piazzi was pregnant. The hospital then petitioned the court to keep the woman on life support until the birth of her fetus, over the objections of her husband and family. The court, in granting the hospital's petition, ruled that the woman lacked the power to terminate life-sustaining medical treatment during her pregnancy even if she had executed a living will. The court also ruled that any privacy rights she may have had during life that allowed her to refuse treatment or terminate her pregnancy were extinguished when she became brain-dead. Instead, the court ruled that public policy in Georgia required the maintenance of life-support systems for a brain-dead mother so long as there was a reasonable possibility that the fetus could develop and survive.[118] The irony of this case is that because the woman was declared dead, the hospital was given the right to keep her alive by maintaining her on life support, regardless of her wishes.

Cryonics

Cryonics is a process in which people who are legally dead are cooled to extremely low temperatures in the hope that future technology will be able to revive and cure them of whatever illness was responsible for their death. Cryonics operates on the belief that there is a difference between clinical death and actual death. Thus, although the legal world speaks of cryonics as the process of freezing dead people and bringing them back to life, proponents of cryonics believe that they are suspending people who have been declared legally dead (because their heart has stopped beating) but who retain sufficient cell structure that they can be restored to biological life and then preserved in that state for future "re-animation."

The technology for revival from cryonic suspension is currently not available, and its very feasibility is subject to serious doubt. Says one skeptic: "Believing cryonics could reanimate someone who has been frozen is like believing you can turn hamburger into a cow."[119] Others, however, are more optimistic and believe that the successes of frozen reproductive technology and nanotechnology make cryonics a real possibility—even if not in the foreseeable future.

In the meantime, more than 150 individuals are in cryonic suspension and a thousand more are members of cryonic institutes awaiting future freezing. In its current state of technological uncertainty, cryonics raises many complex legal issues both for the currently frozen and for those who are contemplating cryonics in their future. These legal issues will multiply exponentially should the technological advances hoped for by the proponents of cryonics occur.

Cryonics began as a movement in the 1960s with the publication of Robert Ettinger's book *The Prospect of Immortality* in 1964.[120] Ettinger suggested that "no matter what kills us, whether old age or disease, and even if freezing techniques are still crude when we die, sooner or later our friends of the future should be equal to the task of reviving and curing us."[121] The first cryonics society was set up in the United States in 1965, and shortly thereafter, James Bedford, a seventy-three-year-old psychology professor, became the first person to be frozen with the intent of future resuscitation.[122] Since that time, cryonics has entered the popular consciousness, becoming a common theme in books, movies, television shows, comics, and video games.[123] Cryonics is also regularly covered in the news media. Cryonics reached a new level of public awareness in 2002 when baseball legend Ted Williams—considered by many to be the greatest hitter of all time—died. At the direction of his son, the body of the Splendid Splinter (as Williams was known) was flown to Arizona to be cryonically preserved. This sparked a court battle among Williams's children, and the publicity associated with the Williams case caused even more people to become interested in cryonics.

Cryonics raises a number of legal issues, including:

- Whether the cryonics industry should be allowed to occur;
- Whether a person's wishes regarding cryonics will be respected;
- Whether a person who wants to be cryonically preserved can maximize his or her chances of successful reanimation by avoiding autopsy and by being frozen as early as possible; and

• Whether a person is able to provide for his or her financial security in the event that reanimation is successful.

Legality

Given the lack of current scientific support for cryonics, some commentators argue that cryonics is a fraud on the public that should not be condoned. A number of jurisdictions outside the United States have taken this position. In the Canadian province of British Columbia, for example, cryonics is explicitly disallowed by a statute.[124] Even where cryonics is not directly prohibited, some countries have effectively disallowed cryonics by requiring that all dead bodies be either buried or cremated. Thus, in a 2006 case in France the top administrative court ruled that a man whose parents' bodies had been frozen for years in the hope that they might one day be brought back to life, had to remove them from a refrigerated crypt in the basement of their château in the Loire Valley to bury or cremate them.[125]

The United States has established a much more favorable environment for cryonics. There are no state or federal statutes outlawing cryonics, and the cryonics industry has even achieved a level of official sanction in some states. For example, a Connecticut statute specifically provides that an individual can direct that his or her body be cryogenically preserved.[126]

Decision-Making Power

The legality of cryonics facilities does not guarantee that an individual's choice regarding cryonic suspension will be upheld. As discussed above, the law in general provides little certainty that a person's wishes regarding his or her body after death will be respected. People have no property interest in their bodies, and the various state statutes allowing people to leave directions regarding their bodies have no mechanism for enforcement. The one area in which wishes regarding the disposition of people's bodies are more likely to be respected is when they are donating part or all of their bodies for organ transplant. The Uniform Anatomical Gift Act provides that an individual's wishes regarding the disposition of their body under the UAGA will be upheld even over family objections.

However, it is not clear whether the UAGA—a statute designed to facilitate organ donations for transplants—applies to cryonic facilities. This has created a new battleground for the proponents and opponents of cryonics.

In California, founding home of Alcor, the largest cryonics facility, the battle took place in the courts. The conflict began in 1980 when the California attorney general issued an advisory opinion that arranging to have one's body placed in cryonic suspension did not meet the requirements of the Uniform Anatomical Gift Act.[127] Based on this opinion the state Department of Health Services (DHS) took the position that burial certificates (required for death certificates) would not be issued for cryonic suspension.

Dick Jones, a Hollywood screenwriter and a member of Alcor, had been diagnosed with AIDS and realized that the position of the DHS meant that only a licensed mortician would be able to remove him from a hospital after a doctor declared him dead. This would mean that he would not be able to be cryonically preserved in a timely manner. Jones and Alcor brought a lawsuit to enjoin the DHS from taking this position.[128] The injunction against DHS was ultimately granted by the trial court and upheld by the California Court of Appeal. However, the decision was based on procedural rather than substantive grounds and therefore has little precedential value for other jurisdictions.[129]

Alcor faced another battle in Arizona—Alcor's base of operation since 1994—this time on the legislative front. In 2004 a bill was proposed specifically providing that cryonics facilities were not eligible donees under the UAGA. After significant lobbying by Alcor and its members, the legislation was withdrawn and no clarifying legislation on this issue has been adopted.[130]

Although the cryonics industry won the battles in California and Arizona, these issues were essentially stopgap measures, and the appropriateness of the cryonics industry has not yet been fully addressed directly by either the legislature or the courts.

Lack of Formal Procedures

The greatest problem for individuals seeking to control their bodies after death is the absence of formal procedures for recording their wishes. This is in sharp contrast to the rules regarding the transfer of property at death. In that realm, the law provides clear rules for expressing one's wishes (typically these rules require that a person's wishes be in writing and signed in the presence of two witnesses who also sign the will). Although the formal requirements for a valid will may in some cases result in people's wishes not being carried out (because the wishes were not presented in the proper form), it more often provides protections for people to state their wishes in ways that they know to be legally meaningful. The lack of these formal procedures for recording wishes regarding one's body makes it difficult for a person to ensure that his or her wishes will be taken into account.

The case of Ted Williams is a good example of how difficult it can be to determine someone's true intent after death when the procedures for stating wishes are not clearly in place. In 1986 Williams wrote a will providing specific instructions for the disposition of his body at death: "I direct that my remains be cremated and my ashes sprinkled at sea off the coast of Florida where the water is very deep."

Nonetheless, when he died in 2002, his son and one of his two daughters had Williams's body sent to Arizona for cryonic preservation. In support of their actions, they submitted to the court a grease-stained scrap of paper dated 2000 that said the following: "JHW, Claudia and Dad all agree to be put into bio-stasis after we die. This is what we want, to be able to be together in the future, even if it is only a chance." The paper had the signatures of Williams and his two children.

Did this paper reflect Williams's true wishes? It is impossible to say. On the one hand, it seemed a clear statement of wishes written after his will; on the other hand, it was written on a grease-stained scrap of paper (not the usual format for a document intended to have legal effect), and it was signed "Ted Williams," the signature he used for autographs, and not "Theodore S. Williams," the signature he used on all official documents intended to have legal effect. It was even suggested by some that Williams could have written his name as an autograph and then the text could have been added around it. If this had been a dispute over property, there would have been legal requirements in place setting standards for when a document would be treated as having legal effect (including the requirement that there be at least two witnesses to the signing who are required to attest to the fact that this person was free from undue influence). Instead, a court in this type of dispute involving physical remains is operating with far less guidance. As one local probate lawyer said, the judge is not bound to agree with the wishes expressed in a will or a note. "The judge is probably going to assess all the equities in the situation, and the wishes of the decedent if they can be determined."[131] In the end, the case was settled without a court determination regarding Williams's true intent, and his body remains frozen at Alcor rather than in the deep waters off the coast of Florida.

Maximizing Chances for Reanimation through Early Preservation

One of the most challenging issues for proponents of cryonics is the ability to maximize the chances of success by preserving individuals before too much damage has been done to their bodies. It is important to remember that although the *law* views the goal of cryonics as bringing someone back to life who was dead, *cryonicists* view their task as the process of preventing death by preserving people who are legally but not *really* dead.[132] As Alcor describes it:

> The object of cryonics is to prevent death by preserving sufficient cell structure and chemistry so that recovery (including recovery of memory and personality) remains possible by foreseeable technology. If indeed cryonics patients are recoverable in the future, then clearly they were never really dead in the first place. Today's physicians will simply have been wrong about when death occurs, as they have been so many times in the past.[133]

Thus, from the cryonicists' point of view, the success of cryonics is dependent on people being preserved (or in the word of cryonicists, "deanimated") at a time when they still have sufficient cell structure to enable "recovery."

Autopsies create significant problems because cryonics is extremely time sensitive and autopsies can delay the cryonics process by days or even weeks, during which time the body undergoes significant degeneration. In addition, the autopsy process itself involves such things as removing and dissecting the brain, which is of course quite destructive to the body.

Under current law, states have broad rights to perform autopsies, and the state's right to perform an autopsy takes precedence over any other wishes of the decedent, including organ donation. The one limitation on this right is that a small number of states provide exceptions for autopsy based on the decedent's religious belief. Alcor and other proponents of cryonics recommend that, where appropriate, their members should take steps to qualify for this exception in order to avoid autopsy. This use of the religious exception (instead of a provision in the law that specifically addresses the desires of those seeking cryonics) is further evidence of how the law has not fully addressed the cryonics industry.

Cryonics can legally be done only on dead bodies—otherwise the cryonics process itself would constitute murder. However, certain diseases, particularly degenerative diseases of the brain, can create significant problems for those wishing to undergo cryonics. One person, Thomas Donaldson, was so concerned with this problem that he went to court seeking the opportunity for early cryonic suspension. Donaldson was a mathematician, computer software scientist, and longtime believer in cryonics who was diagnosed with a fatal brain tumor at forty-three. Because Donaldson's brain tumor was growing rapidly and destroying brain tissue, Donaldson wanted to reserve the option to be cryonically preserved before the brain tumor had done too much damage to his brain. The difficulty with his plan was that it required the assistance of people to administer the cryonic treatment. If this was done while Donaldson was still alive, then the people administering the cryonic treatment could be prosecuted for assisted suicide or murder. To avoid this, Donaldson brought suit against the California attorney general seeking a declaration that he had a constitutional right to premortem cryogenic suspension of his body as well as the right to the assistance of others in achieving this. Although the court was sympathetic to Donaldson's plight, the court of appeals ultimately ruled against Donaldson, stating that he had no constitutional right to assisted death.

Ensuring Financial Future

The final legal question raised by cryonics is whether people are able to provide for their financial future in the event that cryogenic suspension and reanimation ultimately become feasible.

Where there is money to be made, a business usually appears to make it, and this is the case with cryonics. Financial institutions have created entities—called personal revival trusts—designed for people who are being cryonically preserved.

Until recently, the possibility of providing for one's future self in the United States was severely limited by the Rule against Perpetuities. This common law rule existed throughout the United States and limited the length of noncharitable trusts to a period of roughly ninety years (described in the Rule against Perpetuities as "lives in being plus 21 years"). In order to overcome restrictions imposed by this rule, two American entrepreneurs established the Reanimation Foundation, a trust based in the small European principality of Liechtenstein that offers to invest people's money during the period of their cryonic preservation. A promotional brochure touts that a ten-thousand-dollar investment will grow to more than eight million dollars in a hundred years. "You'll be able to buy youth and perfect health for centuries," says the pitch.[134]

Recent changes in the laws now permit these long-term trusts in the United States as well. Motivated by the ability to provide estate tax savings, a number of jurisdictions have repealed the Rule against Perpetuities to allow private trusts to exist in perpetuity (the repeal of this rule is discussed in greater detail in chapter 2). This enables individuals seeking cryonic preservation to establish trusts that will include themselves as beneficiaries in the event that they are eventually reanimated. According to a story in the *Wall Street Journal,* at least a dozen wealthy individuals have created these personal revival trusts designed to allow them to reclaim their riches hundreds or even thousands of years into the future.[135]

Imagining the Unimaginable: What If It Works?

The cryonics industry has been allowed to proceed even though there is no current scientific technology to suggest that its goals of reanimation can be achieved. But what if the promises of cryonics became reality? That would require a rethinking of some of our fundamental legal concepts:

- Most important, life and death would no longer be binary concepts. Instead there would be a third category—not really dead—that the law would have to grapple with.
- What would be the status of surviving family members for the *not re-*

ally dead? Could surviving spouses remarry, or would they be treated as still married, the way that an individual married to someone in a coma would be treated?

- What would happen to the property of the not really dead?
- What would happen to life insurance contracts?
- How would we understand personal identity? Is a severed head that is reanimated and refitted with a new body the same person as the person who died? What if he had none of the memories of the prefrozen person?

If history provides any lessons for the future, one thing for certain is that the law will continue to develop to address these waves of change.

2

CONTROLLING PROPERTY (PART 1):
TRANSFERS TO PEOPLE

If you ask an American about the legal rights of dead people, you will probably get an answer having to do with people's rights to control who gets their property after they die. This right to control the disposition of property at death is central to the American psyche. Although people are often vague in their understanding about many aspects of the law, one thing they do know is that they can write a will that controls who will—and who will not—get their property after they die.

The effect of this ability to control property after death, and the power it conveys to the property owner, is a theme that has been frequently explored in the American arts. Whether in Tennessee Williams's *Cat on a Hot Tin Roof* or Rodney Dangerfield's *Easy Money,* Americans easily recognize the image of would-be heirs currying favor with the future dead to secure an inheritance. In this way, it is well understood that property owners can control much more than just their property; through their right to control the disposition of property at death, they can control the behavior of others during their life. After all, is there any doubt that many May-December unions—marriages between older men and much younger wives—would likely not occur if "December" did not have the power to transmit wealth to "May" at the end of the day?[1]

The right to control the disposition of property at death is often seen as essential to the very notion of private property. It is hard for most Americans to imagine a system of private property that doesn't include a right to control what happens to their property after death. The Supreme Court itself intimated as much when it called the right to transmit property at death "one of the most essential sticks in the bundle of rights that are commonly characterized as property."[2]

Although this connection between property ownership and the right to control it after death may seem inseparable to Americans, this is not the case in other parts of the world. Many countries with strong systems of private property nonetheless distinguish between lifetime and posthumous control of property. Indeed, most other legal systems impose significant restrictions on people's ability to control property after death. Although they may not realize it, Americans have greater rights to control their property after death then anyone else in the world. As one scholar has described it: "As American inheritance law embarks on a new millennium, the scope offered for freedom of testation remains as broad as it has ever been, and it is now indeed a scope without parallel elsewhere in the western world."[3]

The Ability to Disinherit Children

The law of the United States provides that people are generally free to give their property at death to whomever they choose, even at the expense of children and other blood relatives. Although states generally provide some protections against disinheritance for surviving spouses (through community property or elective share rights), America stands virtually alone in providing no protections against disinheritance for adult children. Moreover, in forty-nine of the fifty states (the exception is Louisiana), Americans also have broad latitude to disinherit their minor and dependent children, even if the children will thus become wards of the state.

Part of the explanation for this system stems from the fact that the United States (with the exception of former French colony Louisiana) is a common law country. (Common law countries are those whose laws are based on the common law of England.) Under common law property is owned by individuals (traditionally men) and families have very little claim to the husband/father's property.

In contrast to the United States and other common law countries, many other countries—including most of continental Europe—are civil law countries. Civil law countries view property as something owned by a family unit as opposed to an individual.[4] Individuals in these countries are limited in their ability to control the disposition of their property at death. Civil law countries have statutes which require that a significant portion of the person's estate be given to family members. These statutes, called forced succession statutes, are found in civil codes throughout continental Europe, South America, and Japan. They generally provide protection against disinheritance for the decedent's spouse, children, and grandchildren. Some statutes also provide protection for the decedent's parents and more distant blood relatives. These protections designate a set share for family of between 50 and 80 percent of the decedent's estate, leaving the decedent with freedom to control as little as 20 percent of his or her estate.[5]

Common law countries, including the United States, England, Canada (with the exception of Quebec), New Zealand, and Australia, view property as something owned by individuals, and not families. These countries start with the premise of freedom of testation: the ability of an individual to control the disposition of his or her property at death. As described by one American court: "The right of a testator to make a will according to his own wishes is jealously guarded by the courts, regardless of a court's view of the justice of the chosen disposition."[6] Despite this shared starting point of freedom of testation, however, most common law countries, including England, the mother of our legal system, Australia, and New Zealand, have moved away from total freedom of testation toward granting greater rights to family members through family maintenance statutes. Unlike the forced succession statutes found in civil law countries, these statutes do not provide fixed shares for family members but rather give courts the power to deviate from a person's will to make distribution of a decedent's estate more equitable—at least in the eyes of the judge making the determination.

The English family maintenance statute is a good example of this type of provision.[7] English wills law is the original source of wills law in the United States, and the two systems remain remarkably similar in many respects. Both have a stated ideal of freedom of testation, and both generally share the same formal requirements for executing or revoking a valid will. Yet English law differs from wills law in the United States in one key respect: although both systems provide for freedom of testation, for several decades English law has provided an exception to this right through its family maintenance statute. This statute allows certain people to make claims against a decedent's estate for their support.[8] The right to make such a claim is open to a fairly broad class of individuals, including the decedent's spouse, former spouse, child, current or former stepchild, and any other person maintained wholly or partly by the decedent at the time of the decedent's death. In making a family maintenance determination, an English court is directed to consider numerous factors, including the financial resources and needs that the applicant currently has and is likely to have in the foreseeable future; the size and nature of the decedent's estate; any physical or mental disabilities of the applicant; and any other matter, including the conduct of the applicant or any other person, the court may consider relevant.[9] One court succinctly described its obligation as follows: "In every case the court must place itself in the position of the testator and consider what he ought to have done in all the circumstances of the case, treating the testator for that purpose as a wise and just, rather than a fond and foolish, husband or father."[10]

Thus, in civil and common law countries throughout the world, children are protected against disinheritance by their parent either by being provided a fixed share of the parent's estate (through forced succession statutes) or by being given the right to make an equitable claim against the decedent's estate (through family maintenance statutes). In the United States, however, a disinherited child is left largely without recourse.

The ability to disinherit minor children is particularly surprising when we consider that virtually every state imposes an obligation on parents to support their minor children during life.[11] It is also ironic in that although parents can disinherit their minor and dependent children, these children cannot generally disinherit their parents because they do not have the capacity to make a will. Moreover, in most American jurisdictions, a parent who fails to support his or her child during life can nonetheless inherit from the child in the event of the child's death.[12]

Although disinheritance of minor children is usually not a problem for the child who lives with both parents, it can be a significant problem for children with a noncustodial parent. This is particularly likely to be a problem when the noncustodial parent has remarried and formed a new family. Legal scholar Ralph Brashier has described the situation as follows:

> Increasing numbers of instances are likely to occur such as those in which the noncustodial father bequeathed $1 of his $400,000 estate to an infant daughter from a former marriage; or bequeathed $1 to his infant daughter a few weeks after divorcing the child's mother; or devised everything to his current wife after acknowledging his infant child from an earlier marriage; or left $10 of a $64,000 estate to his infant daughter being reared by his ex-wife.[13]

Children of divorce are not the only ones who are likely to be disinherited: nonmarital children are also susceptible to this fate. The number of nonmarital children has reached epidemic proportions in the United States; almost 40 percent of all children are born out of wedlock. When a paternity action is brought against the putative father of a nonmarital child, he often disputes the claim. If the claim is proven and support is ordered, the father may view the child merely as an unwanted source of debt. However, unlike other creditors, who cannot be written off or "disinherited" by a will, the disinheritance of his child is perfectly permissible.[14]

In recent years, a few cases have upheld probate court decisions to impose child-support obligations against the estate of a deceased parent.[15] These cases, however, do not impose a general obligation on deceased parents to provide for their children; they merely allow probate courts to make such a determination. Moreover, most courts have taken the position that these obligations cannot be imposed without explicit statutory authority from the legislature.[16] To date, only Louisiana imposes a direct obligation on parents to provide for their minor and dependent children upon death.

Many scholars have criticized the American rule allowing disinheritance of children. Some have suggested that states adopt a forced heirship (similar to the rules that exist in civil law countries), or that states adopt a discretionary rule similar to that adopted in England and other common law countries, or that the support obligation for minor children be extended to include the obligation to support children at death.[17] Yet these suggestions have largely fallen on deaf ears.

Louisiana is the only state that provides statutory protection for children in the form of forced heirship.[18] The forced heirship statute protects children against disinheritance by securing for them a minimum share (ranging between 25 and 50 percent) of the decedent's estate that cannot be defeated by will or lifetime transfers.[19] The effect of forced heirship is a statutory system whereby the children of a testator cannot be disinherited unless they do something to "deserve" disinheritance.[20]

Even in Louisiana, however, the trend has been away from family protection and toward individual rights to control property after death. Before 1989, the Louisiana forced heirship statute applied to all children, regardless of their age. That year, however, the Louisiana legislature adopted changes to the forced heirship provisions limiting the protected class of children who are forced heirs to those children under the age of twenty-three or those who, because of mental incapacity or physical infirmity, are unable to care for themselves.[21] These changes were widely perceived as effectively ending forced heirship in Louisiana.[22] Since then, Louisiana has limited its protections to minor and disabled children, and no other state has enacted provisions for the protection of children.[23]

Limited or No Taxation on Transfers at Death

Taxes have the capacity to impose the most direct restrictions on people's ability to control their property after death. These could be in the form of either income or inheritance taxes, which are imposed on the person who receives the inheritance (similar to wages or other income) or estate taxes, which are imposed on the value of a person's assets at death. In either case, a high tax rate could impose significant limitations on a person's ability to control his or her wealth after death. For example, if taxes were imposed at a 77 percent rate (the maximum estate tax rate imposed for more than thirty years during the mid-twentieth century), then a person with a ten-million-dollar estate could control less than $2.5 million after death.

Although income and estate taxes have the *capacity* to reduce people's ability to control wealth after death, this capacity has not been used in recent years. The American federal tax system has never imposed income taxes on gifts and inheritances. Moreover, while estate taxes at one time imposed a limit on the transfer of property at death, these taxes have been significantly eroded in recent years such that 99.5 percent of estates are not subject to taxation.

The income tax system is highly favorable toward inherited wealth. Money received by inheritance is specifically excluded from income taxes. This makes inherited wealth far more valuable than wealth acquired through work, since a person who inherits a hundred thousand dollars will receive the full amount, whereas the person who earns one hundred thousand dollars will receive less than seventy thousand dollars after the government takes its share.[24]

The income tax system provides an additional tax benefit for property transmitted at death that is not available to any other transfers: increases in the value of property between the time the property is purchased and when it is transferred at death are *never* subject to income tax. If a person invests ten thousand dollars and it grows to a hundred thousand dollars, upon sale of the property he or she will have to pay tax on the ninety-thousand-dollar gain. If he or she gives the property away during life, the recipient will be liable for the tax on the gain when he or she sells the property.[25] However, if instead the individual holds on to the property and transfers it at death, the gain is never subject to tax to either the donor or the recipient. The person receiving the property is treated for tax purposes as if he or she had purchased it at the time of death for its full fair-market value. If the person subsequently sells the property, he or she is liable only for taxes on any gain that occurs after the time of inheritance. The entire ninety-thousand-dollar gain that occurred before death is never taxed.[26]

Because of this favorable treatment in the income tax system for inherited wealth, the only way that these transfers are subject to taxes in the United States would be through the estate tax system. Estate taxes, however, have been drastically reduced in recent years, imposing only minimum restrictions on the vast majority of American taxpayers.

Estate Taxes Yesterday and Today

Most taxes are enacted with the primary purpose of raising the revenue necessary to run a government. Estate taxes are unusual in their twofold purpose: in addition to raising revenue, estate taxes were also enacted for the purpose of limiting large concentrations of wealth.

The United States is a very wealthy country, but the wealth is distributed in a highly disproportionate way. This disparity in wealth is far greater than the disparities in income. Thus, whereas the highest paid 1 percent earn 20 percent of the country's income, the wealthiest 1 percent own more than 34 percent of the country's wealth. Beyond the top 1 percent, wealth continues to be extremely concentrated, with the wealthiest 10 percent of the country owning more than 70 percent of the country's wealth. As for the vast majority of the public, 80 percent of households together own less than 16 percent of the nation's wealth (with a shocking 40 percent of households owning less than 1 percent of the nation's wealth).[27] Wealth concentration is a problem from the point of view of economic health of the country; studies have consistently found that high concentrations of wealth correlate with poor economic performance of the country as a whole.[28] Moreover, when great wealth is held in the hands of a few, the affluent may gain too much power, significantly harming the democratic process.[29] As Supreme Court Justice Louis Brandeis said: "We can have concentrated wealth in the hands of a few or we can have democracy. But we can't have both."[30]

The problem of wealth concentration first came to the fore with the rise of industrialization in the late nineteenth century. In the Gilded Age, or the Robber Baron Era, as some call it, a relatively small number of businessmen amassed huge personal fortunes, often through questionable business practices. People whose names are still well known today—Andrew Carnegie, John James Astor, Henry Ford, J. P. Morgan, Andrew Mellon, John D. Rockefeller—acquired levels of wealth that had previously been unheard of in the relatively new United States. In doing so, they challenged America's self-identity. Previously, the United States had defined itself as a place of equal opportunity, standing in stark contrast to the stratified European countries with entrenched aristocracies.[31] This creation of the American aristocracy added a new dimension to the American myth of unlimited opportunities and raised the question as to how society should address the issue of concentrated wealth.

An early thinker on this question was, perhaps appropriately, one of these new aristocrats, Andrew Carnegie. Andrew Carnegie was an original self-made man. A poor immigrant from Scotland, he began working at age sixteen as a telegraph messenger boy after only four years of formal education. Through astute investments and strong business acumen as well as ruthless union busting, Carnegie eventually founded and developed Carnegie Steel Company, a highly successful corporation that later became U.S. Steel, the largest and most profitable industrial enterprise in the world. When Carnegie sold his company to J. P. Morgan in 1901 for $480 million (of which Carnegie was entitled to half), he possessed the greatest fortune ever amassed by an American.[32] After retiring, Carnegie devoted the last fifteen years of his life to large-scale philanthropy, including funding more than three thousand libraries in forty-seven states. By the time he died, Carnegie had given away more than $350 million (more than four billion dollars in today's money). At his death, the last thirty million dollars was likewise given to foundations, charities, and pensioners. Carnegie's rags-to-riches story is common enough in American history, and even the transformation from industrialist to philanthropist is a path that others have taken. What makes Carnegie unique is that on top of these many accomplishments, he was a prolific writer and public commentator. From 1882 to 1916, Carnegie published eight books, sixty-three articles, and ten public addresses in pamphlet form.[33] Carnegie's writings were published in all the leading journals, and his down-to-earth writing style made him popular with people of all ages and backgrounds.

In one of his most famous essays, "The Gospel of Wealth," Carnegie addressed one of the most pressing issues of his time: the divide between wealthy and poor, which in the wake of the Industrial Revolution was greater than it had ever been in American history. According to Carnegie, this divide was not altogether bad, because the creation of wealth ultimately served to the betterment of the masses, such that the least wealthy people lived better than the wealthiest of their forebears. However, Carnegie noted, even if great divisions of wealth were inevitable and perhaps beneficial, this did not mean that the wealthy should be able to pass their riches down to the next generation. As he explained:

> Why should men leave great fortunes to their children? If this is done from affection, is it not misguided affection? Observation teaches that, generally speaking, it is not well for the children that they should be so burdened. . . . [I]t is no longer questionable that great sums bequeathed oftener work more for the injury than for the good of the recipients. Wise men will soon con-

clude that, for the best interests of the members of their families and of the state, such bequests are an improper use of their means.[34]

Carnegie believed that the best thing for wealthy people to do was to give away their money to good causes during life, but he also realized that not everyone would follow his precepts, and for those who failed to commit their excess wealth to philanthropy, Carnegie was a strong proponent of heavy estate taxes: "Of all forms of taxation, this [the estate tax] seems the wisest. Men who continue hoarding great sums all their lives, the proper use of which for public ends would work good to the community, should be made to feel that the community, in the form of the state, cannot thus be deprived of its proper share. By taxing estates heavily at death the state marks its condemnation of the selfish millionaire's unworthy life."[35]

Although Carnegie was a big proponent of federal estate taxes (and testified in favor of them in Congress), estate taxes were not a regular part of the federal tax system in Carnegie's time. Instead, estate taxes had previously been enacted only for short periods in order to raise funds for war efforts.[36] President Theodore Roosevelt proposed the first permanent estate tax in 1906, but the tax was not enacted until the nation was on the brink of war in 1916. Unlike previous versions of the estate tax, however, this tax was not repealed when war ended, and it formed the basis for our current estate tax.

As enacted, the estate tax was relatively modest, imposing maximum rates of 10 percent (this highest rate applied only to estates that exceeded five million dollars). Over the years, however, and particularly beginning in the 1930s, estate tax rates began to increase dramatically, ultimately reaching a maximum rate of 77 percent, which applied from 1941 to 1977 (some commentators refer to these years as the golden age of the estate tax).[37] President Ronald Reagan began reducing estate tax rates in earnest in 1981. Even then, however, the maximum rates were still imposed at 55 percent. That changed with the enactment of the 2001 Tax Act, which at least temporarily effectively eviscerated the estate tax.

For many years the estate tax served as an effective antidote to large concentrations of wealth. Wealth concentration in the United States had hit a historic high in 1912, the end of the Gilded Age, when the top 1 percent of Americans owned 56.4 percent of the national wealth. Through the imposition of estate taxes and the development of other policies that promoted the growth of a middle class, such as the GI Bill, federal mortgage assistance programs, and loans to small businesses, the wealth held by the top 1 percent decreased to under 20 percent by 1976.[38]

Beginning in the 1980s, however, this trend reversed, and wealth concentration again became a prominent feature of the American economic landscape. Thus, in 2004, the wealthiest 1 percent of Americans controlled more than a third of the nation's wealth. Given current tax policies, the trend is likely to continue in the direction of further wealth concentration.[39]

Wealth distribution is particularly skewed when race is factored in. In 2004, the median white household had ten times the wealth of the median black household ($118,000 for whites and $11,800 for blacks).[40] The difference in average wealth is much greater than what would be accounted for by the difference in household income.[41] Several studies suggest that disparities in inheritances may play a large role in perpetuating this racial divide. One study from the late 1990s found that whites were expected to inherit an average of sixty-five thousand dollars, whereas blacks were expected to inherit on average only eight thousand dollars. In addition, whites were ten times as likely as blacks or Hispanics to receive a six-figure inheritance.[42] A more recent study found that the racial gap in inheritance is likely to be much greater for the baby boomer generation than it has been for prior generations: the mean inheritance for white baby boomers is expected to be $125,000, whereas the mean inheritance for black baby boomers is expected to be only sixteen thousand dollars.[43] This disparity in inheritance means that the racial gap in overall economic status is expected to increase even while earning gaps are being reduced.[44]

The estate tax was thrown into upheaval with the election of President George W. Bush in 2000. Bush made elimination of the estate tax a top priority in his administration, and with a largely Republican Congress and extremely effective lobbying by opponents of the estate tax, the tax's demise was set in place. Opponents of the estate tax effectively shifted debate away from the problems of concentration of wealth by calling the tax the "death tax," suggesting that the tax hits people at their most vulnerable time.

The result of this upheaval was "EGTTRA," the 2001 Tax Act. Under this law, the estate tax has been gradually repealed between 2001 and 2009, with the amount that each person can pass free of tax (the exemption amount) increasing from $675,000 to $3.5 million in 2009 and maximum rates falling to 45 percent. The law then provides for an elimination of the estate tax in 2010. As the law currently stands, however, in order to meet budgetary requirements, the estate tax elimination does not extend after the year 2010. Instead, after 2010, the exemption amount will revert to $1 million and the maximum estate tax rate will be 50 percent. Although no one expects this "here today gone tomorrow" law to remain in effect, no one knows whether the estate tax will ultimately be retained or scrapped altogether.

The Cost of Failing to Tax Transfers of Wealth

By failing to tax transfers of wealth to either the donor or the recipient, the United States is giving up an opportunity to raise revenue that could be used for a number of purposes, including reducing taxes for less well-off individuals or funding programs that would be beneficial for the country at large. For example, if inherited income was simply taxed the same as other income (such as wages or lottery winnings), it has been estimated that it would have raised roughly sixty billion dollars in 2009 alone.[45] Moreover, although few of us like to pay taxes, the imposition of an estate or inheritance tax is less painful than other taxes because the property is essentially in between owners.

In addition to the lost revenue, there is another, more serious problem. Failing to tax transfers of wealth at death promotes and nurtures an aristocratic class—individuals with enormous amounts of wealth and power achieved not because of their talents or effort but solely because of the luck of their birth.

Why should Americans be concerned about this type of wealth? After all, some might argue that wealthy individuals are beneficial to a community because they use fewer public resources and often give to the community in the form of charitable donations. The problem of the wealthy is not their existence but their disproportionate power in government. Like water to a fish, the effect of wealth on legislation in the United States is almost impossible to see owing to its sheer magnitude.

The wealthy exercise their power over the legislative and elective process in a number of ways. Most directly, the wealthy are able to make donations to candidates, political action groups, and lobbyists to support their causes as well as to finance their own runs for political office. Even without making direct expenditures, the wealthy have power from politicians *knowing* that they have the excess funds to donate.[46] This power is evidenced in the number of multimillionaires in Congress as well as the type of legislation that has been supported in recent years that often benefits the wealthy.

Thomas Jefferson was particularly concerned about this type of aristocracy holding too much power. As he wrote late in life to John Adams on 28 October 1813:

> For I agree with you that there is a natural aristocracy among men. The grounds of this are virtue and talents. . . . There is also an artificial aristocracy founded on wealth and birth, without either virtue or talents; for with these it would belong to the first class. The natural aristocracy I consider as the most precious gift of nature for the instruction, the trusts, and government of society. And indeed it would have been inconsistent in creation to have formed man for the social state, and not to have provided virtue and wisdom enough to manage the concerns of the society. May we not even say that that form of government is the best which provides the most effectually for a pure selection of these natural aristoi into the offices of government? The artificial aristocracy is a mischievous ingredient in government, and provision should be made to prevent its ascendancy.

The famed French observer of nineteenth-century America Alexis de Tocqueville also warned about the dangers to democracy of excessive inherited wealth: "What is most important for democracy is not that great fortunes should not exist, but that great fortunes should not remain in the same hands."[47]

In our time Jim Repetti has pointed out how the problem of wealth in the political process gets worse over time: "Wealth passed from generation to generation magnifies political power. It is one thing to deal with a more powerful person than yourself; it is another to consider that your children will have to deal with the children of the powerful person, and that your grandchildren will have to deal with her grandchildren."[48]

The strength of the democratic system is that governmental policies are at their root supposed to be policies of the people being governed. However, when there are gross disparities in wealth, there is more likely to be a mismatch between the interests and perspectives of those who govern and those who are governed. Everybody sees the world from their own perspective, and the wealthy are no less likely to do so than anyone else. The top 1 percent of Americans who control more than a third of the country's wealth have very different concerns than the 80 percent who together control just 15 percent of the nation's wealth. Wealthy Americans often have privatized education for their children, privatized security for their homes, and privatized medical care through no-insurance, concierge doctors. It is unreasonable to expect that they will have the same level of interest in devoting resources to high-quality public education, effective police and fire protection, and affordable medical care—let alone rights for workers and the unemployed.

What about all of the charitable giving by the wealthy? Although much good can be done through charitable spending, it is a different type of good than that which can be done through government expenditures. Charitable dollars do not fund necessary public expenditures, such as the costs of national defense or Social Security. In addition, private dollars cannot create programs that have a truly transformative effect on society, such as the GI Bill and investment in public education. Moreover, decisions about how charitable dollars are spent are made by the wealthy individual instead of through the political process. In this way, reliance on private charity as opposed to public tax revenues further undermines the strength of the democratic form of government.[49]

Controlling from the Grave

During life, people with property can use it to exert their control: they can pay people to do things, they can fund political campaigns, they can purchase land for preservation or development and art for private or public display, and they can give money to organizations whose work they support.

After death, a person with property can continue to exert control only if the law provides a mechanism for his or her wishes to be carried out. In American law, a person's ability to exert specific control over property after death is made possible because of the existence of the legal entity known as the trust.[50]

The term "trust" is commonly used—particularly in reference to rich people and tax-saving devices—but less commonly understood. Simply put, a trust is a way of owning property. Unlike regular ownership, in which the property owner has both the ability to control the property and the right to the economic benefit of the property, a trust divides ownership of property between the trustee (the person who has legal title to the property and therefore the ability to exert all legal rights over the property, such as buying, selling, and leasing) and the beneficiary (the person or purpose for whose benefit all actions with respect to the trust property must be taken). The person creating the trust leaves instructions to the trustee regarding how the property should be disbursed. This is usually done in a written document called the "trust instrument." The trust instrument sets the term of the trust and can provide for successor trustees and successor beneficiaries. In this way, a trust can last long after the end of the life of the person who established the trust (as well as the lives of the original trustee and beneficiary).

The law recognizes two types of trusts: private trusts and charitable trusts. Charitable trusts are not for the benefit of particular individuals but instead are for the promotion of a particular purpose. Unlike private trusts, which until recently were subject to strict time limits, charitable trusts have long been allowed to exist in perpetuity. Charitable trusts are said to be a favorite of the law, and a number of provisions in the law support this characterization. Charitable trusts raise many issues that are discussed in chapter 3. This chapter focuses on the use of private trusts to control wealth long after the person establishing the trust has died.

A private trust is one that is established for the benefit of particular individuals. Private trusts are commonly used to control wealth long after the property owner has died. Traditionally private trusts have been strictly limited in terms of their duration. Recent changes in the law, however, have allowed private trusts to last as long as 350 years, a thousand years, and even in perpetuity. The private trust does not exist in civil law countries. Although these countries have some comparable vehicles for a person to impose his or her wishes after death, they are significantly more limited than the flexibility that is available under the American trust. Moreover, in the United States trust law has developed to grant greater controls to the dead than exist in other common law countries. In England, for example, the adult beneficiaries of a private trust can terminate the trust even if the purpose for which the settlor has established the trust has not been accomplished.[51] By contrast, in the United States, a court will continue to enforce the wishes of the settlor as established in the trust regardless of the wishes of the beneficiaries in terminating the trust.[52]

A private trust can be used for many purposes. It has been said that "the purposes for which trusts can be created are as unlimited as the imagination of lawyers."[53] And whatever one's view of the imagination of lawyers in general, trusts have indeed been established for many purposes. Some of the common uses of trusts are to provide management of money for minor children or for people who lack financial sophistication. However, private trusts can also be used to induce behavior by imposing conditions on their receipt and to keep wealth intact for future generations.

Conditional Bequests

During life, people can use their wealth to induce behavior in others. They can give money to someone for quitting smoking, for marrying a particular person, for breaking off an engagement, or even for divorcing their spouse. Provided that the desired behavior is not illegal (such as paying someone to murder your spouse or paying for sex), these agreements are recognized and enforced.[54] What about after the person has died? To what extent will the law allow people to continue to exert control in this way?

American law has been very liberal in terms of allowing individuals posthumous control over the behavior of others through the use of conditional trusts. The theory that courts have consistently espoused in enforcing these provisions is that since no one has the right to demand an inheritance, the person giving the property can generally impose whatever conditions he or she chooses. In upholding these provisions courts have regularly noted that since the heirs could have been disinherited entirely, they cannot complain about having conditions imposed on their bequests. As one court described it: "It must be borne in mind in all such instances that the legacies and devises were acts of bounty merely. The testator was free to withhold them altogether, or to subject them to conditions, whether sensible or futile. The gift is to be taken as made or not at all."[55]

The only limitations that courts put on these conditions is that they cannot be "illegal" or "against public policy." The restriction against illegal conditions means that presumably a court would not enforce a provision that said that the beneficiary was obligated to kill the testator's former boss in order to receive the inheritance. Although the rule against illegal conditions is often cited by courts and is a favorite of law professors, it is rarely applied since there are no actual cases on record involving illegal conditions.[56]

Thus, the only relevant restriction on conditional bequests is that a court will not enforce a condition that is "against public policy." In theory this public policy exception could severely restrict conditional bequests, for the term is infinitely malleable. In practice, however, this has not proven to be much of a limitation; American courts have generally been loath to use their authority to restrict these conditions, seeing it as outside their bailiwick. As one court described it: "[A] testator has the right to grant bequests subject to any lawful conditions he or she may select. Beneficiaries of a testamentary instrument have no right to testamentary bequests except subject to the testator's conditions, and it is generally not the role of the court to rearrange those bequests or conditions in keeping with the court's sense of justice."[57]

One area where people often seek to impose conditions is with regard to marriage. Although the right to marry is constitutionally protected, courts have consistently upheld bequests conditioned on either forbidding the beneficiary from marrying or requiring the beneficiary to marry someone of a particular group on the theory that these provisions do not restrict the beneficiary's right to marriage; they only restrict the beneficiary's right to inherit.[58]

Courts have been particularly understanding of husbands conditioning their wives' inheritance on remaining unmarried after the husband's death. As one court saw it: "It would be extremely difficult to say, why a husband should not be at liberty to leave a homestead to his wife, without being compelled to let her share it with a successor to his bed, and to use it to hatch a brood of strangers to his blood."[59]

When it comes to children, testators have been more interested in requiring them to marry someone of a particular religion or background, and courts have generally been supportive of these controls as well. Thus, in one case, in order to inherit his share of his father's estate, a son was required to marry "a Jewish girl both of whose parents were Jewish" within seven years of his father's death.[60] In another case the testator's daughter was required to marry a "man of true Greek blood and descent and of Orthodox religion" before receiving her inheritance.[61]

Sometimes a testator is interested not just in preventing or requiring a new marriage but instead in ending an existing marriage. The official position of courts is that conditions designed to encourage divorce are against public policy, and accordingly courts have refused to enforce these conditions in several cases.[62] This rule is easily circumvented, however, because even though courts will not enforce conditional bequests where the testator intended to encourage divorce, they will enforce such conditions if the testator intended to provide support in the event of divorce. As one court described it: "A condition to a devise, the tendency of which is to encourage divorce or bring about separation of husband and wife, is against public policy, and void. However, if the dominant motive of the testator is to provide support in the event of such separation or divorce, the condition is valid."[63]

This exception is particularly easy to take advantage of because courts tend to give testators the benefit of the doubt when it comes to determining intent. In one case the testator gave money to his nephew on condition that at the time of the testator's death, the beneficiary "is not married to his present wife." Although the court noted that conditions intending to encourage divorce or separation were against public policy, the court said that this provision did not violate this rule and enforced the restriction. In doing so, the court explained:

> It is of no consequence that the settlor objected to his nephew's marriage and was unfriendly and hostile to his wife . . . and that

several years before he said to his nephew: "If you get rid of her I will make you richest of the family." The intention of the settlor and the validity of the condition is to be ascertained from the unambiguous language used, which cannot be enlarged or restricted by extrinsic evidence. The wording of the gift holds out no inducement to the nephew to separate from his wife. The condition having been valid, the failure of respondent to bring himself within it deprives him of any share in the trust estate.[64]

Another surprising area where testators can exert their control is over the beneficiaries' practice of religion. Freedom of religion is a cornerstone of our constitution. Yet courts have consistently upheld bequests that are conditioned on the beneficiary either practicing or refraining from practicing a particular religion. For example, in one case a woman was entitled to receive income from the trust only "so long as she lives up to and observes and follows the teachings and faith of the Roman Catholic Church and no longer."[65] Another testator required that the grandchildren would inherit only if they were "members in good standing of the Presbyterian Church."[66] Yet another testator conditioned his son's inheritance on attending "regular meetings of worship of the Emmanuel Church near the village of Cashton, Wisconsin, when not sick in bed or prevented by accident or other unavoidable occurrence."[67]

In a culture that values religion, these conditional bequests may be understood as being based on the theory that encouraging people to be more religious is not against public policy. However, this justification does not explain why courts also regularly allow conditional bequests that require the beneficiary to *refrain* from practicing a particular religion. Thus, in one case the testator's daughter received her inheritance only if at the age of thirty-two she proved conclusively to the trustee that "she has *not* embraced, nor become a member of, the Catholic faith nor ever married a man of such faith."[68] In another case the court allowed a trust that required the testator's brother to "withdraw from the priesthood in the Roman Catholic Church" in order to receive his inheritance.

These conditional bequests are not without their critics. Jeffrey Sherman has argued that such "posthumous meddling" should not be allowed because such bequests are against public policy. However, to date, Sherman's arguments have fallen on deaf ears. Nothing suggests that either courts or legislatures have any interest in curtailing this type of dead hand control, as it is known.[69]

Dynasty Trusts

One reason courts have been liberal in allowing people to impose their wishes after death through the use of trusts is that private trusts have traditionally been subject to strict time limits. From the founding of the Republic through most of the twentieth century, the Rule against Perpetuities has limited the duration of private (as opposed to charitable) trusts to approximately ninety years, after which time the dead hand must cede control to the living. All of this changed in the 1980s when, in a confluence of events, states began to abandon this long-standing rule, making way for perpetual private trusts (marketed to the public as "dynasty trusts"). Dynasty trusts create opportunities for people to exert their will after death in ways never before possible. More troubling, although these trusts operate largely outside the public view, like spores in a horror movie, they are poised to fundamentally transform the face of the United States by creating a new aristocracy made up of individuals who have access to large amounts of untaxed wealth to meet their every need and desire while being immune from claims of creditors.

THE PURPOSE AND HISTORY OF THE RULE The Rule against Perpetuities is a common law rule that was first enunciated in England in 1682 in the Duke of Norfolk's Case.[70] The English colonists brought the Rule (as it is known)[71] with them to the New World, where it was ultimately adopted by all fifty states. The purpose of the Rule is to limit people's ability to control property into the future. This was particularly problematic at a time when wealth consisted largely of land and was therefore a finite resource (imagine if we had to live today in a world where all the land was subject to strictures imposed in the seventeenth century). However, the Rule against Perpetuities was also concerned with people's ability to dictate uses of property for future generations whom the settlor could know nothing about. In 1955 Lewis Simes, the great scholar of trust law, described the twofold value of the Rule against Perpetuities as follows:

> First, the Rule against Perpetuities strikes a fair balance between
> the desires of members of the present generation, and similar de-

sires of succeeding generations to do what they wish with the property which they enjoy. . . . But in my opinion, a second and even more important reason for the Rule is this. It is socially desirable that the wealth of the world be controlled by its living members and not the dead. I know of no better statement of that doctrine than the language of Thomas Jefferson, contained in a letter to James Madison, when he said: "The earth belongs always to the living generation. They may manage it then, and what proceeds from it, as they please during their usufruct [lifetime use]."[72]

The Rule has a simple goal but a convoluted method, and it has achieved mythic proportions for lawyers and law students alike.[73] The Rule limits the length of time a property owner can control the use of his or her property, through a trust or otherwise. Rather than stating the limit in terms of years, however, the Rule operates in a more Delphic manner, stating that "no interest is good unless it must vest, if at all, not later than twenty-one years after some life in being at the creation of the interest."[74] Thus, under the Rule, a person can only control property for so long as he or she "lives in being plus 21 years." The theory of the Rule is that a person should be able to impose restrictions only on people whom he or she knows plus the period of minority for the next immediate generation. After that, the person must give up control so that the property can be held free and clear of control by future generations.

One reason for the Rule's infamy is the potent combination of harsh and unforgiving punishment for violation combined with complex technical rules that are easy to run afoul of. If a provision violates the Rule (in that it would be possible for it to continue past "lives in being plus 21 years"), then the effect of violation is that the gift is void from the beginning. Moreover, in determining whether it is possible for an interest to continue past the prohibited period, judges do not limit themselves to probable or even likely scenarios. Rather, if any situation can be imagined that could yield the result of violation of the rule, then the gift fails. For example, if property is to be held in trust until twenty-five years after the settlor's death, then that trust would violate the Rule because it is *possible* that everyone in the world could die the day after the settlor, and then the trust would last longer than "lives in being plus 21 years." This type of fantastic analysis gave rise to judges imagining a variety of far-fetched situations in order to void different bequests, including the fertile octogenarian (women giving birth in their eighties) and the unborn widow (the possibility that one of the beneficiaries would eventually marry someone who was not yet born at the time that the trust became effective).[75] The Rule was so complex that one court found that a lawyer who violated the Rule could not be held liable for malpractice because it would be unfair to expect an attorney to fully understand its contours.[76]

By the mid-twentieth century, there began to be widespread agreement that the Rule against Perpetuities was in need of fixing, and states began adopting statutes that would make the Rule easier to comply with. The most widely adopted was the Uniform Statutory Rule against Perpetuities (USRAP). This statute provided that a trust would be valid if its terms were limited to ninety years. Although technical problems with the Rule were thus well on their way to being resolved, these solutions were soon eclipsed by larger changes brought about by market forces.

THE UNDOING OF THE RULE It began with a trickle. The Rule against Perpetuities was first repealed in Idaho in 1957, then in Wisconsin in 1969 and South Dakota in 1983. The gush began in 1995, when Delaware repealed its Rule against Perpetuities. Within the next ten years Alaska, Arizona, Colorado, Illinois, Maine, Maryland, Missouri, Nebraska, New Hampshire, New Jersey, Ohio, Rhode Island, and Virginia had all repealed their version of the Rule.[77] Other states enacted more modest provisions, merely extending the time limit allowed for dead hand control from the traditional period provided by the Rule (or ninety years provided under USRAP) to 360 years (in Florida and Nevada) or a thousand years (in Utah and Wyoming).

What brought about this sudden change of heart such that a rule that had survived more than three hundred years was suddenly being abandoned in droves? This was particularly surprising in light of the fact that the more technical difficulties of the Rule had already been addressed by statutory changes in a significant number of states. Like many changes in law that occur in a capitalist system, the repeal of the Rule against Perpetuities was heavily influenced by market forces.

To understand these changes, it is important to grasp the tax world in which they arose, namely the estate tax and the generation-skipping transfer tax. As discussed above, a primary purpose of the estate tax was to limit concentrations of wealth by imposing a tax on property as it passed from one generation to the next. This is best understood by considering the case of a great-grandparent who had a hundred million dollars of wealth and an estate tax system that imposed taxes at a 50 percent rate. Theoretically, as the property passed from great-grandparent to grandparent, the hundred million dollars would be reduced to fifty million; as it passed from grandparent to parent, it would be reduced to twenty-five million, and as it passed from parent to child it would be further reduced to twelve and a half million dollars. In this way, the estate tax was conceived as a tax that would limit the power of inherited wealth as one got further from the person who first produced the wealth. However, although the estate tax was supposed to operate this way, after a half-century of experience, it became clear that the estate tax was not always accomplishing its goals. Instead, many of the country's wealthiest families were able to significantly reduce the effect of the estate tax by establishing long-term trusts that effectively evaded its application.

Evolutions in the tax system occur as a result of a complicated dance between the government and tax advisers. The government creates a plan to raise revenue, and tax advisers respond with mechanisms for their clients to avoid the government's plan. The government then responds by closing these avenues (called loopholes by the government), and the tax advisers try to find other ways around, and so the dance continues.

In the estate tax world, the dance began with the original enactment of the estate and gift tax system. Tax planners responded by having their clients transfer their property into long-term trusts that provided financial benefits to the client's beneficiaries while shielding the assets from taxation in the beneficiaries' estates.[78] Thus, in the above example, although the hundred million dollars from the great-grandparent would be subject to tax when it was transferred into the trust (reducing it to fifty million dollars), thereafter it would not be subject to tax until such a time that it was held outright by the beneficiaries (which typically occurred at the latest time permitted by the Rule against Perpetuities). John D. Rockefeller used this tax-planning technique in setting up elaborate trusts for his descendants that still benefit members of the Rockefeller family today.

These generation-skipping trusts became standard practice for families of substantial wealth. Indeed, as a practical matter, they were *only* available to those families wealthy enough to keep their assets locked up in trust. Thus, those who should have been most directly affected by the gift and estate taxes were often effectively shielded from taxation for several generations (limited only by the Rule against Perpetuities).[79]

To close this loophole, Congress enacted an additional tax system, called the Generation-Skipping Transfer tax, or GST tax. The GST tax was designed to address this problem by imposing an additional tax (equal to the maximum federal estate tax rate) on transfers that skip a generation. Thus, if someone tried to avoid estate taxes by transferring property to a multigenerational trust, then the GST tax would nonetheless apply as each generation's interest terminated.

The GST tax was originally enacted in 1976, but its complexity led Congress to repeal the 1976 version and replace it with a new GST tax in 1986. Although both versions of the GST tax addressed the underlying problem, the two approaches had one significant difference. Namely, the 1986 version included an exemption from the GST tax of a million dollars per person (which has since been raised to $3.5 million), which could be used by taxpayers to make generation-skipping transfers. By including this exemption, Congress created a marketing bonanza for banks and trust companies and encouraged wealthy individuals to establish generation-skipping trusts.

Congress did not go into this with its eyes closed. Raymond Young, then the chairman for the Generation-Skipping Transfer Tax Subcommittee of the Boston Bar Association, warned of this result in his 1984 testimony:

> We are obliged to point out to you that if [the 1986 GST tax] is adopted . . . , it will be an inducement to generation-skipping. You will have more generation-skipping than you ever had under pre-1976 law, and there will be a greater erosion of the tax base, because you will have the banks, lawyers, financial planners, and all others saying, here you are, this is a specially created opportunity for you. Congress has said you can take $1 million, put it aside, no generation-skipping tax.[80]

Young's testimony was truly prophetic. Since the enactment of the 1986 GST, generation-skipping trusts have become a standard component of estate planning for wealthy clients. Yet, one thing that even Young didn't foresee was how bank and trust companies, in a bid to attract more generation-skipping trusts into their states, would convince their local legislatures to enact legislation to make these generation-skipping trusts even more valuable to their clients. The two modes that were most commonly used were repealing the state's Rule against Perpetuities, so that federal transfer taxes could be avoided for longer periods, and repealing the state's income taxes on trust assets from out of state.

South Dakota, an early repealer of the Rule against Perpetuities, saw the opportunity for growth of its trust business and began marketing to those outside the state. "You don't have to live in South Dakota to benefit from a South Dakota Legacy Trust," went one ad campaign.[81] When Delaware repealed its Rule against Perpetuities in 1995, the legislative history made clear that legislators were motivated by a desire to increase the state's trust business.[82] Other states quickly followed suit.

One of the most transparent examples of business driving changes to state law occurred in Alaska. Jonathan Blattmachr—a New York lawyer and one of the best-known estate-planning attorneys in the country—was reportedly on a fishing trip with his brother Douglas in Alaska when they came up with the idea of making Alaska the premier state in the country for trust business. In 1996 Douglas Blattmachr formed the Alaska Trust Company. At the same time Jonathan Blattmachr drafted trust-friendly legislation—including the repeal of the Rule against Perpetuities—that the brothers successfully lobbied the Alaska legislature to enact. Although some might feel a sense of unease at this direct link between business and legislation, it is touted on the web site of the Alaska Trust Company, which explains its history as follows: "Alaska Trust Company was founded in 1996 by the financial and estate planning experts that helped create Alaska's advantageous and liberating trust laws. . . . Alaska Trust Company gives you access to the friendliest trust laws in the United States no matter where you live. You do not have to be an Alaskan resident, or even visit the state, to benefit."

Were these repeals effective in terms of encouraging the growth of states' trust business? Most decidedly, yes. Empirical studies have shown that on average, a state's abolition of the Rule increased its reported trust assets by 20 percent (the Alaska Trust Company boasts assets of four billion dollars). It has been estimated that more than a hundred billion dollars in trust fund assets has moved to take advantage of the abolition of the Rule.[83]

THE MARKETING AND SOCIAL COSTS OF DYNASTY TRUSTS As predicted, dynasty trusts have become part of a standard estate plan for wealthy individuals. This has been tremendously profitable for banks and other financial service companies, which can generate large fees administering these long-term trusts. They are also advantageous for individuals seeking to impose their wills on generations to come, since private trusts can now be established in perpetuity. At the same time, the growth of dynasty trusts has the capacity to impose significant costs. First, dynasty trusts harm some of the very beneficiaries that they are designed to protect. Second, and more important, dynasty trusts have the capacity to impose significant costs on the rest of society.

Dynasty trusts are designed to benefit a person's heirs for generations to come. Undoubtedly, many of these individuals will be quite happy to learn that they have been well provided for by their ancestor. Ironically, however, dynasty trusts can also impose harm on beneficiaries. Many wealthy people, including Andrew Carnegie and Warren Buffet, believe that it is not in their children's best interest for them to be given so much wealth that they don't need to work. As Carnegie said: "It is no longer questionable that great sums bequeathed oftener work more for the injury than for the good of the recipients." To address this concern, many wealthy people choose to give their money to charity rather than to their children. And yet, dynasty trusts take this decision-making authority away from parents because the ancestor settling the trust—and not the parent—decides how much wealth their descendants will get at each generation.

More significant, dynasty trusts have the capacity to impose considerable societal harm. Dynasty trusts are commonly structured to leverage the GST tax exemption to shelter far more assets then ever imagined by those who enacted the original regime. As enacted, the GST tax allowed each individual to transfer one million dollars free of tax. As part of the evisceration of the estate tax put in place by President George W. Bush in 2001, this amount was increased to $3.5 million for each individual (seven million dollars for a married couple). Although these amounts are substantial in their own right, they represent only a small percentage of the wealth that can and is being transferred under the stated GST exemption. The reason for this is that financial and tax advisers have mastered ways of leveraging the exemption to be worth far more than it appears on its face. One way of doing this is by using money in a dynasty trust to purchase life insurance policies. One article marketed to practitioners explains how a one-million-dollar GST exemption can be leveraged to a fifty-million-dollar legacy through the use of life insurance.[84] In another method individuals use funds in a dynasty trust as start-up capital for a business enterprise or to purchase a minority interest in an existing family business (where such interests can be valued at a significant discount).[85] When the business is owned by a trust, it is forever exempt from transfer taxes, regardless of how large the business becomes.

Dynasty trusts avoid taxes only as long as the money stays in the trust. For this reason, it might initially appear that these trusts would naturally die of their own accord as money is distributed to beneficiaries. Estate planners, however, are drafting dynasty trusts to avoid this result by providing that the trust will purchase property for use by the beneficiaries instead of making outright distributions. One practitioner's treatise describes the method as follows:

> It is not expected that the trustees would make distributions to the beneficiaries. To preserve corpus, rather than making distributions outright, the trustees would be authorized to acquire assets for the use of the beneficiaries. For example, if one of the transferor's children or grandchildren wished to acquire a vacation home, the trustees of the trust would purchase the home and allow the child or grandchild to use the home. The home, however, would always remain an asset of the trust and, therefore, any appreciation in the value of the home would inure to the benefit of the future beneficiaries of the trust. Moreover, because funds were not distributed to the child or grandchild to purchase the home, the home would not be includable in the child's or grandchild's estate on his or her death.[86]

The same treatise goes on to explain how these trusts should also be drafted to allow beneficiaries to purchase businesses with trust assets, thereby allowing further tax-free growth.

These perpetual, ever-growing trusts provide advantages and protections for their beneficiaries that are not available to anyone else. First, there are tax advantages: for so long as property is retained in the trust, it is not subject to estate or GST taxes. Second, beneficiaries are not subject to taxes on property purchased for their use and enjoyment (this differs from the situation for working people, in which the provision of housing or other benefits are taxed as imputed income). Last, distributions from the trust are also received tax-free because gifts are specifically excluded from the income tax system.

Perhaps even more surprising than the tax avoidance is the fact that these trusts are also commonly drafted to insulate the beneficiaries from claims of creditors and ex-spouses. This is typically accomplished through inclusion of a so-called spendthrift clause, which provides that trust assets cannot be reached by a beneficiary's creditors. Spendthrift clauses have been prohibited as against public policy in England, but they are widely accepted in the United States. Thus, these beneficiaries are free to act as recklessly as they like, knowing that their money is forever protected for themselves and their heirs.

Mindful of concerns that this magnitude of wealth may not be good for the maturation of beneficiaries, wealthy individuals have been encouraged to pass on their values through the use of incentive provisions. As described in one article: "In traditional trusts, beneficiaries receive money at a certain age, but in incentive trusts, heirs must reach milestones or take actions. For example, children might receive a $25,000 bonus when they graduate from college or marry. Or they might receive funds matching money they earn."[87]

Incentive trusts may appear to provide a good counterbalance to the negative effect of wealth, yet these types of provisions raise their own issues, particularly in light of the length of term of these trusts. For example, although some provisions may appear benign and even socially beneficial (such as education and marriage), as we saw when we looked at conditional trusts, there is no reason to think that testators will always be so high-minded: conditional bequests are allowed that control a wide range of behaviors, including choice of marriage partner, practice or avoidance of religion, and requirements as to personal dress. Moreover, while a testator's views on these issues may be tolerable as applied to the testator's children and grandchildren, the problems become more apparent when imagining their impact on future generations. Even in a state that revises its Rule against Perpetuities modestly (allowing trusts to exist for only 350 or a thousand years), permitting such incentive trusts is the equivalent of enforcing trust provisions today that were created by people who lived in the latter part of the seventeenth century or the eleventh century. This becomes even harder to imagine in the case of perpetual trusts: forever is a very long amount of time indeed.

3

CONTROLLING PROPERTY (PART 2): TRANSFERS FOR CHARITABLE OR OTHER PURPOSES

Rather than giving their money to people, individuals sometimes want to commit their wealth to fulfill a particular purpose. During life there are virtually no limits to what people can do with their money: they can give to political candidates, support the work of educational and religious institutions, build monuments to themselves or others, and promote causes they believe in. People can also do things with their money that others might consider strange or inappropriate. They can use dollar bills as cigarette paper and smoke them, buy perfectly good houses and tear them down, and spend lavishly on their pets. Indeed, short of supporting activities that are against the law, people are free to spend their money in whatever manner they choose.

And after death? While during life the law takes a largely hands-off approach to people's choices, this is not true for transfers after death. Indeed the law's treatment of postmortem transfers for a purpose is highly disparate depending on the particular purpose being promoted. Whereas transfers for charitable purposes are strongly encouraged and given financial benefits, other types of transfers fare less well. Some purposes are tolerated only in limited circumstances, while still others are forbidden outright as against public policy—even when these same actions would have been allowed during the person's life.

Transfers for Charitable Purposes

People commonly seek to direct their wealth to charitable purposes at death. There are a number of reasons for this. First, many people have a general desire to benefit society. Charitable transfers at death enable people to fulfill those desires at a time when they know they no longer need the resources for their own support. In addition, donating to charity is a way of expressing one's identity.[1] Finally, some charitable bequests are inspired by a desire to secure a form of immortality. For some religious believers, this can come in the form of preserving their souls (by financing good deeds or the saying of Masses), while for others it can come in the form of buildings and programs at universities and other large charitable institutions or their own private foundation. Rockefeller, Ford, Carnegie, Stanford, Harvard, Yale, MacArthur, Pew, and Duke are all names known to us today because of the charitable organizations that live on doing the work originally inspired by the founder.

The desire to make—or remake—one's identity has no doubt provided a strong inspiration for much charitable giving. Thus, it was reputedly the erroneous publication of an obituary that prompted Alfred Nobel to establish his eponymous charitable foundation. Nobel had made his fortune from the development of dynamite and other armaments. When his brother was killed, a newspaper mistakenly thought it was Alfred and published his obituary, which began, "Le marchand de la mort est mort" (The merchant of death is dead), and continued, "Dr. Alfred Nobel, who became rich by finding ways to kill more people faster than ever before, died yesterday."[2] Shortly after this obituary was published, Nobel rewrote his will to devote the bulk of his estate to create the Nobel Foundation, which grants annual prizes to those who have conferred the greatest benefits to humanity.[3] These annual prizes have enabled Nobel's name to be linked with some of the most respected individuals of each generation.

The law governing charitable giving has undergone a dramatic transformation throughout U.S. history. From the early days of the Republic through much of the nineteenth century, transfers for charitable purposes were viewed with suspicion, and the law was at times actively hostile to these transfers. This aversion was expressed in two forms: state statutes (called "mortmain," meaning dead hand in French), which limited individuals' ability to make transfers to religious and other charitable organizations, and court decisions that prevented individuals from establishing perpetual charitable trusts.

Since the beginning of the twentieth century, however, the treatment of charitable bequests has enjoyed a dramatic turnaround. First, mortmain statutes have been virtually eliminated. Second, individuals are free to establish trusts lasting forever for any charitable purpose they choose. Most significantly, today these transfers are actively subsidized by the federal government in the form of tax benefits—at least for the wealthiest Americans.

What Is Charitable?

The law provides special benefits to transfers for charitable purposes. This raises the question: What makes a purpose charitable? Although "charitable," in its colloquial sense, refers to being generous to those in need, in the context of the law, the word has both a more particular and a broader meaning. First, for a transfer to be considered charitable, it must be to an organization with a charitable purpose. Thus, even though a bequest to a needy family might be "charitable" in the colloquial sense, it would not qualify as a charitable bequest because it is not for the benefit of an organization. Second, the concept of charitable within the law is also broader than the colloquial meaning because it need not be for the benefit of the needy. Indeed, the law considers a broad range of purposes that are considered beneficial to society in general to be charitable.

There is no clear definition of what constitutes a charitable purpose. The most commonly cited guidance is the Restatement of Trusts.[4] It provides a somewhat circular definition that a purpose is considered charitable "if its accomplishment is of such social interest to the community as to justify permitting the property to be devoted to the purpose in perpetuity." The restatement lists the range of purposes that have been recognized as charitable, including "the relief of poverty, the advancement of education and of religion, the promotion of health, the accomplishment of governmental or municipal purposes, and other purposes the accomplishment of which is beneficial to the community."[5]

Although some of these categories, such as education and religious organizations, are fairly well delineated, the catchall category "beneficial to the community" is more difficult to apply since what one person sees as beneficial to the community another might see as serving no such purpose. Consider the English case involving the Irish playwright George Bernard Shaw.

Shaw was interested in simplifying the written English language.[6] He wrote many of his manuscripts in the form of shorthand developed by Sir James Pitman, and he thought it would be useful to have an English alphabet that was phonetic and therefore simpler to use. To that end, Shaw left the residue of his estate (he began receiving significant royalties after his play *Pygmalion* was adapted by Alan Jay Lerner and Frederick Loewe into the tremendously successful musical and movie *My Fair Lady*) to a trust to develop a new phonetic English alphabet of forty letters in which each letter could be pronounced in only one way. Shaw believed that this new English alphabet would be extremely useful to writers and readers of the English language, but the court did not agree. In *In re Shaw* the court ruled that the Shaw alphabet trust was neither for the advancement of education nor beneficial to community and therefore was not a charitable trust.[7]

The concept of what constitutes a charitable purpose is often deeply affected by when it is being evaluated. In 1865, for example, the Massachusetts highest court ruled that a bequest to trustees (two of whom were Lucy Stone and Susan B. Anthony) "to secure the passage of laws granting women, whether married or unmarried, the right to vote, to hold office, to hold, manage and devise property, and all other civil rights enjoyed by men" was not charitable because its purpose could not be accomplished without changing laws.[8] Just about one hundred years later another court ruled that a trust to help further passage of the proposed Equal Rights Amendment (a proposed amendment to the U.S. Constitution providing equal rights regardless of sex) did have a valid charitable purpose.[9]

Questions about what constitutes a charitable purpose are not merely relics of history. More recently, a Texan named Charles Walker left a handwritten will that included an ingenious plan to make millionaires of all Americans. The will provided as follows:

> I hereby direct my Executor to sell [a parcel of land] for cash and to invest the proceeds in safe and secure tax-free U.S. government bonds or insured tax-free municipal bonds. This trust is to be called the James Madison Fund to honor our fourth President, the Father of the Constitution. The ultimate purpose of this fund is to provide a million dollar trust fund for every American 18 years or older. At 6% compound interest and a starting figure of $1,000,000.00, it would take approximately 346 years to provide enough money to do this.[10]

Although it recognized that Walker's intent was generous and benevolent, the court nonetheless ruled that the purpose was not "charitable" because "Walker intended nothing more than to financially enrich the American public" and there was no evidence that this would promote the social interest of the community.[11]

Despite these cases, the overall trend is for courts to be liberal in their determination of what constitutes a charitable purpose. In recent years, charitable status has been recognized for trusts with purposes as diverse as promoting excellence in quilting and preserving Huey military aircraft (its members will educate all generations in the history of the American-made Huey in Vietnam and its fifty years of service in the U.S. military).

The law of charitable trusts is all or nothing: if the purpose is recognized as charitable, the trust will receive the myriad of benefits conferred on charitable trusts, regardless of the relative societal value afforded by the trust. The legal scholar Lewis Simes described this phenomenon as follows: "There are no degrees of charitableness. Exactly the same privileges and immunities are accorded in the creation of the great foundations, whose purposes are sometimes stated to be to distribute the income for the benefit of mankind, as are accorded to a bequest to maintain a hospital for ailing Siamese cats."[12] On the other hand, if the purpose is not recognized as charitable, not only will the special benefits be denied, but in most cases the bequest will fail altogether owing to the requirements imposed on private trusts.[13] If the bequest fails, the property generally passes to the donor's next of kin.

Charitable Bequests in the United States: A Historical Perspective

Charitable giving in America was formerly not treated with the deference it is today. The law was deeply ambivalent about charitable giving—particularly in perpetuity—and imposed a number of restrictions. These restrictions took two forms: mortmain statutes, which limited transfers at death to religious and charitable organizations, and court cases, including from the Supreme Court, which set aside individuals' attempts to devote their property to charitable purposes in their wills.

Mortmain Statutes

From the nineteenth century through much of the twentieth century, it was common for states to have mortmain statutes allowing spouses and children to set aside deathbed gifts to religious organizations and other charities. Mortmain statutes restricted charitable giving by either disallowing charitable bequests in wills made shortly before the donor's death or by prohibiting charitable gifts in excess of a designated fraction of the donor's estate.

Mortmain statutes were ostensibly enacted to address concerns that as people get closer to death, they may be inclined to direct their estates to a religious or charitable organization to ensure their eternal salvation. Mortmain statutes were thus considered to fulfill two purposes: to protect testators (as well as their rightful heirs) against the testator's improvidence, and to deter clergy and representatives of other charitable organizations from exerting undue influence on the frail and elderly.[14] Religious bigotry was undoubtedly also associated with these statutes. As historian Lawrence Friedman has described it, "A faint odor of anti-Catholicism also hung over these laws—the fantasy of the evil priest, extorting ransom for the Church from the dying man, as the price of absolution."[15]

Beginning in the 1970s some states' mortmain statutes began to be successfully challenged on a variety of constitutional grounds, and other states simply repealed their mortmain statutes. As a result, the only mortmain statute still in effect today is one in Georgia. The Georgia statute has very narrow applicability. It applies only to wills made within ninety days of the person's death where the decedent is survived by a spouse or descendants and the gift to charity is in excess of one-third of the dece-dent's estate. The Georgia statute is further limited in that it does not apply to the extent that the value of the estate exceeds two hundred thou-sand dollars.[16]

The Precarious History of Charitable Trusts

People often seek to devote their property to a particular chari-table purpose. Beginning in the sixteenth century English law allowed this through the device of the charitable trust—the technical term for the situation where a person gives property to another with instructions to use that property for a particular charitable purpose. Charitable trusts could be established either during life or at death through a bequest in a will. After the Revolutionary War, the newly created American states were in an upheaval over whether to continue to follow the law of England or create a new American law that better reflected the values of the new de-mocracy. The charitable trust, associated as it was with privilege, the dead hand, and massive wealth held in perpetuity, was viewed with particular suspicion.[17] There was particular concern about problems that could arise from religious establishments controlling large amounts of property in perpetuity. As James Madison wrote:

> But besides the danger of a direct mixture of Religion and the civil Government, there is an evil which ought to be guarded ag[ain]st in the indefinite accumulation of property from the ca-pacity of holding it in perpetuity by ecclesiastical corporations. . . . The growing wealth acquired by them never fails to be a source of abuses. A warning on this subject is emphatically given in the example of the various Charitable establishments in G.B. [Great Britain] the management of which has been lately scrutinized. The excessive wealth of ecclesiastical Corporations and the mis-use of it in many Countries of Europe has long been a topic of complaint. In some of them the Church has amassed half perhaps of the property of the nation. . . . In the U.S. there is a double motive for fixing limits in this case, because wealth may increase not only from additional gifts, but from exorbitant advances in the value of primitive one. In grants of vacant lands, and of lands

in the vicinity of growing towns & Cities the increase of value is often such as if foreseen, would essential control the liberality confirming them.[18]

These concerns were not without merit. In addition to the experiences of Great Britain (where before the English Reformation the Church owned much of the land), the history of Mexico provides an example of difficulties that can arise when organizations with perpetual life acquire large amounts of land in developing countries.

Catholic missionaries came to Mexico with the sixteenth-century Spanish conquistadors. The clergy played a strong role in the communities, and it was not uncommon for people at death to give large amounts of their land to their local churches. Over the centuries, the power of the Catholic Church grew along with the Church's landholdings; by the mid-nineteenth century, the Church owned half of the land in Mexico. This extensive land ownership by the Church meant that there was less land available for private ownership, which in turn inhibited the development of a strong middle class.[19] The extraordinary wealth of the Church also enabled it to play a powerful role in the country's political evolution. The Church actively opposed Mexico's independence from Spain.[20] Only after Church land was seized by President Benito Juarez in the mid-nineteenth century did the Church's political power begin to diminish.

The issue of the validity of charitable trusts in American law came about in the wake of the American Revolution when many state legislatures struck all British statutes from their laws. These included the English Statute of Charitable Uses, which had explicitly authorized charitable trusts. Although some states subsequently enacted their own statutes, others did not, leaving open the question of whether bequests for charitable purposes would be recognized. The issue at last came before the United States Supreme Court in 1819 in the case of *Philadelphia Baptist Association v. Hart's Executors*.[21]

Silas Hart, a Virginia resident who died in 1795, had made a bequest in his will to the Baptist Association of Philadelphia. Hart's will directed that the bequest was to be used to educate Baptist youth for the ministry. Virginia was one of the states that had struck all British laws without enacting its own statute authorizing charitable trusts. The question before the Court was whether Hart's wishes would be given effect. Although the Court noted that Hart's philanthropic intentions would have been upheld under the English Statute of Charitable Uses as well as under prior Virginia law, it ruled that the statute had fallen in December 1792, when the state legislature struck all statutes and acts of Parliament from Virginia law. Because there was no statute on point authorizing charitable trusts, the bequest was set aside and the property was instead given to Hart's heirs. The opinion was written by Chief Justice John Marshall, with Justice Joseph Story concurring.

Although this decision was rather technical, it was backed by the reputations of Marshall and Story, two of the most influential jurists of the era, and had an enormous impact on lower courts, which for the next hundred years regularly set aside charitable bequests.[22] In this era courts were generally suspicious of allowing "every private citizen the right to create a perpetuity for such purposes as to him seem good."[23] In one of the most notorious cases, a New York court set aside a four-million-dollar bequest from Samuel Tilden (former governor of New York and almost-president of the United States) to establish the Tilden Trust to fund a public library in New York City.[24] The New York courts refused to give effect to the bequest and instead awarded the money to Tilden's heirs.[25] The public outcry over this decision was so strong, however, that the New York legislature responded by enacting the Tilden Act in 1893 validating charitable trusts in New York.[26]

The ongoing power of the *Hart* decision was particularly surprising in light of the Supreme Court's reversal of itself, twenty-five years later, in the case of *Vidal v. Girard's Executors,* holding in 1844 that a charitable trust could be upheld even in the face of statutes abolishing English law.[27] Yet not until the early twentieth century were charitable trusts generally recognized throughout the United States.[28]

What explains this shift in legal opinion about the validity of charitable trusts? On a doctrinal level, the shift has been explained as a result of a deepening understanding of English legal history and the technical question of whether charitable trusts were the product of English statutory law (which had been repealed in many states after the Revolution) or principles of equity and common law (which continued to apply). This explanation, however, fails to take into account the larger social context in which this transition occurred.[29]

The late nineteenth century was a time when individuals in the United States began amassing wealth at levels never before seen in history. At the same time, it was an era of growing public awareness of larger societal ills, particularly those suffered by immigrants in the rapidly expanding American cities. In the end, the combination of societal problems in need of resources and the possibility of devoting a portion of this growing private wealth to the problems of the day outweighed earlier concerns about the unfettered growth of perpetual charitable organizations. This transformation was also eased by the simultaneous development of another entity with perpetual existence: the corporation. The public's growing familiarity with perpetual organizations in the context of business also likely served to decrease people's apprehension regarding perpetual charitable trusts.

Charitable trusts today have both legal and social acceptance. Few worry about the societal costs of charitable trusts and large dynastic wealth owned by nonprofit organizations (even though the wealth of the Bill and Melinda Gates Foundation is greater than that of many countries). Charitable trusts are touted as win-win institutions, serving the dual purposes of providing resources to address social problems as well as giving people a way to "live on" after death. Despite this appeal, charitable trusts are not without their issues, particularly those raised by the fact that they exist in perpetuity and that they are heavily subsidized through the tax system.

Charitable Bequests Today: Immortality Achieved

The contemporary law of charitable bequests affords unequaled opportunity for Americans to live on after death through charitable bequests. Mortmain statutes limiting charitable gifts at death have been virtually abolished, and the charitable trust is accepted throughout the country, allowing "every private citizen the right to create a perpetuity for such purposes as to him seem good."[30]

Charitable bequests enable people to live on in a variety of ways:

• In some religions, a person's *soul* can be helped into eternal life through particular human activities, such as the saying of Masses in his or her name. People regularly seek to give money to religious organizations to say Mass in their names. Although these types of bequests have been

outlawed in England for a long time, they have been consistently supported under American law as a valid charitable bequest.

- A person's *name* can be given continued existence through charitable naming opportunities. A common benefit of charitable giving is
that the donor's name is publicly associated with some aspect of the
charitable institution. Sometimes these naming opportunities are for
aspects of an institution's physical plant—everything from a building
to a wing to a room down to a single brick in a walkway. At other
times the naming is of a particular program or a whole institution.
Regardless of the size of the gift, the law of contracts enforces these
agreements and plays a role in ensuring perpetual advertisement of the
person's generosity.

- A person's *charitable plan* can be given continued existence through
the charitable trust. Whether the plan is general in nature (for example, for the betterment of humanity) or specifically targeted (for example, to provide scholarships to children from a particular background or geographic area or provide resources to cure a particular
disease), the law of charitable trusts promises to enforce a donor's plan
for as long as he or she likes, even in perpetuity.

The Law of Charitable Trusts

A charitable trust is created when a donor transfers property to a
trustee (a trustee is simply the name of the individual or entity charged
with holding trust property and carrying out the donor's wishes) and directs the trustee to use the property to carry out a charitable purpose.
The charitable work could be performed by the charitable trust itself, but
just as commonly the charitable trust directs money to other charitable
organizations. A charitable trust can be established during life or at death;
regardless of when it is established, however, the law of charitable trusts
enables people to continue to exert their will long after their bodies cease
to exist.

Two defining features of the law of charitable trusts make them particularly effective in allowing a donor to achieve a form of immortality: the
focus on enforcing the donor's intent, as opposed to serving broader societal values, and the ability for charitable trusts to exist in perpetuity.

FOCUS ON DONOR INTENT The defining principle infusing American law of charitable trusts is to give effect to the donor's wishes as expressed in the donor's charitable plan. (This is different from English law, in which there has been greater emphasis on the use of trusts to promote social welfare.)[31] This value is effectuated through the multitude of technical rules governing charitable trusts—from the obligations of the trustees to the ability (and lack of ability) of courts to amend charitable trusts.

The primary obligation of the trustee is to carry out the donor's intent—regardless of whether the donor is dead or alive and regardless of whether the money could arguably be put to better uses. If the trustee fails to carry out its duties, the state attorney general is authorized and obligated to ensure that the donor's intent is carried out. Each state attorney general's office maintains a charities division devoted to this purpose. Thus, if a donor transfers ten million dollars to a bank as trustee and directs the bank to invest the money and use the income to provide scholarships for people of a particular community, then the bank is legally obligated to do so. If the trustee tries to do something with the money other than providing scholarships pursuant to the donor's plan, then the attorney general's office is obligated to step in and enforce the donor's wishes.

The donor's plan is supported even when the money could arguably be put to better uses. In one case, a donor named Beryl Buck left her estate in trust to benefit "the needy in Marin County, California and for other non-profit charitable, religious, or educational purposes in that county." In the period after her death, a number of things happened that caused the trustee to request expanding the beneficiaries of the trust to include other counties in the San Francisco area. First, a growth in the affluence of Marin County (which had become known as the hot-tub capital of the world) diminished the number of "needy" in the county. Second, because of a corporate buyout, the size of the Buck Foundation grew exponentially in value from nine million dollars, when the trust was established, to three hundred million dollars. The trustees took the position that had the donor known about this posthumous surprise, she would have spread her bounty more widely. In rejecting the trustees' request, the court ruled that as long as it was possible to carry out the donor's wishes as expressed in her trust, the trustee was obligated to do so, regardless of whether there were other, more compelling uses for the money.

American law further acts to fulfill the donor's wishes by giving courts limited authority to modify the terms of a trust (rather than allowing the trust to fail). Under the doctrine of "cy pres" (the term derives from the French expression "cy-près comme possible," as near as possible), if a charitable purpose becomes "impossible, impracticable or illegal" to fulfill, and if the donor expressed a general charitable intent, then a court can modify the terms of the trust to put in place an alternate scheme that will carry out the donor's original charitable scheme as nearly as possible. A classic example of a trust that might be suitable for cy pres would be where a donor has created a trust to provide care to individuals who suffer from a particular disease and the disease is subsequently eradicated. Under American law, if the court finds that the donor had exhibited a general charitable intent, then a court could put in place an alternate charitable scheme that would most closely approximate the donor's original intent. In our example this might be a diversion of the assets to be used for the care of individuals suffering from a similar illness.

The application (and nonapplication) of cy pres is done with a constant focus on the donor's intent regardless of how much time has passed. This focus on donor intent occurs both for purposes of determining whether to apply cy pres and then again for purposes of implementing cy pres.

Under American law, a court will modify a charitable trust only if the donor is found to have had a general charitable intent. This differs from English law, which allows a trust to be modified under cy pres without proving a general charitable intent on the donor's part.[32] The effect of this more restrictive application of cy pres is that assets of a charitable trust in the United States are more likely to be returned to the donor's heirs, sometimes providing them a surprise windfall long after the donor has died.

A case in point is the Supreme Court case of *Evans v. Abney*. This case arose from a controversy surrounding the will of Augustus Bacon, a four-term senator from Georgia. In 1911 Senator Bacon wrote a will transferring property in trust to the City of Macon, Georgia, for the creation of a public park—to be known as "Baconsfield," in memory of his sons—for "the sole, perpetual, and unending use, benefit and enjoyment of white women, white girls, white boys and white children of the City of Macon."[33] In his will, Bacon explained the reason for the racial limitation:

> I take occasion to say that in limiting the use and enjoyment of this property perpetually to white people, I am not influenced by any unkindness of feeling or want of consideration for the Negroes, or colored people. On the contrary I have for them the kindest feeling, and for many of them esteem and regard, while for some of them I have sincere personal affection. I am however without hesitation in the opinion that in their social relations (white and negro) should be forever separate and that they should not have pleasure or recreation grounds to be used or enjoyed together and in common.

Fifty years later, public sentiment had changed drastically, and what had seemed unremarkable in Bacon's time—racially segregated parks—became socially and legally unacceptable. The racial restriction was challenged, and in 1966 the Supreme Court ruled that the park could not continue to be operated on a discriminatory basis. This left open the question of what was to happen to the park. The two options available were to amend the trust under the doctrine of cy pres to remove the racial restriction, or to not apply cy pres, in which case the trust would fail and the parkland would be given to Bacon's living heirs. In deciding whether to apply cy pres, the Court did not consider public policy or the equities of the case but rather limited its inquiry to what its understanding was of whether Senator Bacon (who had been dead for more than fifty years) would have preferred. In exploring Senator Bacon's intent, they did not imagine what he would have wanted had he continued to live to contemporary times but rather what he would have wanted in 1911 had he known that the restriction would not have been upheld. The Court decided that Senator Bacon was more interested in his bigotry then he was in making a charitable bequest to the City of Macon and therefore that the trust should fail and the property should revert to his heirs. After the heirs received the property, they sold it to developers, and Baconsfield became an office park.[34]

The donor's wishes also play a dominant role when courts apply cy pres. Under American law, the doctrine of cy pres requires that if a charitable trust needs to be modified (because the original purpose becomes impossible to fulfill), then the modification must be made as close as possible to the donor's original intent. The effect of this is that when courts do apply cy pres, they tend to authorize only the most minor changes to the donor's plan. The cost of protecting donor's intent has often been gross inefficiencies since courts are directed to focus primarily on the donor's intent and to pay only minimal attention to current societal needs.

A good example of some of the inefficiencies that can result from the narrow application of cy pres is the trust established by Milton Hershey (the founder of the Hershey chocolate company) and his wife, Catherine, "for the residence and accommodation of poor white male orphans." Hershey's wife died in 1919, and in his grief over his wife's death, Milton Hershey transferred thousands of acres of land and all of his stock in the chocolate company (then valued at more than sixty million dollars) in trust for the creation of the orphanage.[35]

After the trust was established, problems arose. Orphanages were no longer seen as the best way of providing care to children who had lost their parents, and racial and gender restrictions were no longer socially acceptable. Although cy pres was used to address some of these issues (changing the purpose from an orphanage to a residential school and lifting the race and gender restrictions), another problem could not be so easily addressed. The size of the Hershey Trust grew from sixty million dollars at the time of its inception (already an enormous amount) to more than eight billion dollars in 2008.[36] It has been hard for the trustees to spend all of the trust income on the residential school. Even after spending ninety-three thousand dollars a year to educate, house, clothe, feed, and nurture each of its twelve hundred students, the school still had a reserve fund of more than $850 million from all the money it could not spend over the years.[37] In 1999 a request was made to spend twenty-five million dollars of the accumulated income to create an institute to train teachers in educating at-risk children. In denying the request, the court ruled that even though the trust was consistently unable to spend its annual income, the money could not be spent for another purpose because "our discretion is not unfettered and, if exercised, must be within the limits approximating the dominant intent of Hershey."[38]

INTENT IN PERPETUITY Not only is the law of charitable trusts devoted to fulfilling the donor's intent, but it is committed to doing so in perpetuity. The law allows the donor's wishes to be carried out in perpetuity in a number of ways. First, charitable trusts are not subject to the Rule against Perpetuities, the common law rule that traditionally limited the duration of noncharitable trusts to approximately ninety years. Until late into the late twentieth century (when many states began abolishing their Rule against Perpetuities), charitable trusts provided the *only* opportunity for Americans to control their property after death without being subject to a time limit. Thus, in 1955, Lewis Simes, the great scholar of trust law, described the charitable trust as follows: "It gives full scope to the control of the dead hand, far beyond that which is possible anywhere else in the law. By this device, the vanity of the dead capitalist may shape the use of property forever."[39]

Second, donors are encouraged to impose their wishes in perpetuity by establishing private charitable foundations. Private charitable foundations are a form of charitable trust that do not engage in charitable activities directly but merely hold money for disbursal to other organizations that do. In addition, a private foundation is typically funded by a small number of people. The Bill and Melinda Gates Foundation, the Ford Foundation, and the John D. and Catharine T. MacArthur Foundation are examples of some of the largest private charitable foundations, but there are many smaller ones as well. Private charitable foundations, like other charitable trusts, are not subject to any time limitation.

Federal tax law encourages donations to these perpetual entities by granting an up-front deduction for the full amount of money transferred to the foundation, even though there may be a significant lag time before the money is eventually disbursed for charitable purposes. How much lag time is there between the time of the deduction and the time of the distribution for charitable use? A lot. These organizations are required to spend only 5 percent of their asset value each year. Moreover, in meeting this 5 percent minimum, a private charitable foundation is allowed to count trustees' salaries and other administrative expenses as part of its charitable spending. Thus, if the assets of the foundation are valued at a million dollars, the trustees are only obligated to spend fifty thousand dollars each year. Moreover, since administrative expenses, including trustees' salaries, also count toward this minimum, if the trustees are making an annual salary of thirty thousand dollars and the trust has ten thousand dollars of other administrative expenses (such as rent or legal or accounting fees), the trust need only commit ten thousand dollars of trust assets to charitable purposes. Yet the full one million dollars still qualified for the charitable deduction at the time of transfer.

The value of the 5 percent rule is that, provided the charitable foundation can earn at least 5 percent in income, the principal can be preserved and the organization can be assured of perpetual life. The cost of this perpetual life, however, is that fewer dollars are being currently spent on charitable purposes. In 2003 legislation was proposed that would have required foundations to devote the full 5 percent of asset value toward true charitable expenditures, barring foundations from counting operating expenses (such as rent and salaries) toward the 5 percent minimum. If that law had passed, then a trust with a value of a million dollars would have been required to devote the full fifty thousand dollars to charity in order for transfers to that trust to qualify for the charitable deduction. But private foundations successfully fought this legislation by arguing that its effect would be to destroy perpetual life for charitable trusts. They argued that if they earned only 6 percent each year and had administrative expenses of 2 percent, then the obligation to spend 5 percent on charitable giving would reduce their capital and could eventually deplete their resources to nothing. The lobbying was successful, and the bill didn't pass.

Problems with Perpetual Charitable Trusts

The perpetual charitable trust is such a presence in our society that it is hard to imagine any other type of charitable giving. However, periodically throughout both English and American history, people have questioned the value of establishing charitable trusts in perpetuity. Legal scholar Evelyn Brody has traced some of these critics.[40]

The Victorian novelist Anthony Trollope illustrated the corruption and waste that can ensue from perpetual charitable trusts in *The Warden* (1855), which concerns a medieval trust established in 1434 for the support of twelve retired wool-carders (a wool-carder was a person who cleaned wool in preparation for spinning). Although the value of this trust grew enormously over the years, the purposes for which it had been established did not—particularly since wool-carders had been replaced by machines in the eighteenth century. In fact, as Trollope illustrates, through time the true beneficiaries were the trustees who received management fees far greater than the amount afforded the so-called beneficiaries of the trust.[41]

> In the year 1434 there died at Barchester one John Hiram, who had made money in the town as a wool-stapler, and in his will he left the house in which he died and certain meadows and closes near the town . . . for the support of twelve superannuated wool-carders, all of whom should have been born and bred and spent their days in Barchester; he also appointed that an alms-house should be built for their abode, with a fitting residence for a warden, which warden was also to receive a certain sum annually out of the rents of the said butts and patches. . . . From that day to this the charity had gone on and prospered—at least, the charity had gone on, and the estates had prospered. Wool-carding in Barchester there was no longer any; so the bishop, dean, and warden, who took it in turn to put in the old men, generally appointed some hangers-on of their own; worn-out gardeners, decrepit grave-diggers, or octogenarian sextons, who thankfully received a comfortable lodging and one shilling and fourpence a day, such being the stipend to which, under the will of John Hiram, they were declared to be entitled. . . . Such was the condition of Hiram's twelve old men when Mr Harding was appointed warden; but if they may be considered as well-to-do in the world according to their condition, the happy warden was much more so. The patches and butts which, in John Hiram's time, produced hay or fed cows, were now covered with rows of houses; the value of the property had gradually increased from year to year and century to century, and was now presumed by those who knew anything about it, to bring in a very nice income; and by some who knew nothing about it, to have increased to an almost fabulous extent.

In 1880 the English reformer Courtney Kenny wrote an essay outlining the fundamental problems with perpetual charitable trusts. Perpetuity, Kenny observed, creates the paradox "that whilst charity tends to do good, perpetual charities tend to do evil." The main problem with perpetual endowments for charities is that "the inevitable tendency of endowed charities to be either neglected or perverted as time runs on. Hence it is utterly inexpedient to narrow their resources during their youth, for the purpose of augmenting their superfluities in their decrepitude."[42]

In the United States, the arguments against perpetual charitable endowments were made most forcefully by Julius Rosenwald, who has been described as "the greatest 20th century donor you've never heard of."[43] Julius Rosenwald made his wealth as one of the early owners and developers of Sears, Roebuck and Company. Like many other titans of wealth, Rosenwald became a philanthropist late in life. Through his philanthropic work, Rosenwald was responsible for the establishment of more than five thousand schools to serve rural black communities in the South. He also donated large sums of money to the University of Chicago and was the major contributor to Chicago's Museum of Science and Industry (and resisted attempts to have the building named the Rosenwald Museum). Unlike other philanthropists of his day, however, Rosenwald was adamantly opposed to making his charitable grants in perpetuity. When he gave two million dollars to the University of Chicago, he did so only on the condition that the money not be added to the university's endowment (the university instead created a special account for the Rosenwald donations, which were exhausted by 1942). When he established his private foundation, he included a provision in the trust that all assets must be spent within twenty-five years of his death. In the end, the Rosenwald Fund had donated over seventy million dollars to public schools, colleges and universities, museums, Jewish charities, and black institutions before funds were depleted in 1948.

In addition to engaging in philanthropy himself, Rosenwald had another personal mission: to discourage other philanthropists from tying up their philanthropic bequests in perpetuity. He laid out his arguments in a series of articles beginning with an article published in the *Atlantic Monthly* in 1929 called "Principles of Public Giving." This essay has been described as the most important article written by a philanthropist since Andrew Carnegie wrote "The Gospel of Wealth" in 1889.

In urging his fellow philanthropists not to tie up their wealth in perpetuity, Rosenwald directly took on people's desire to preserve their reputations in perpetuity:

> I am certain that those who seek by perpetuities to create for themselves a kind of immortality on earth will fail, if only because no institution and no foundation can last forever. If some men are remembered years and centuries after the death of their last contemporaries it is not because of endowments they created. Harvard, Yale, Bodley, and Smithson, to be sure are still on men's lips. But those names are now not those of men but of institutions. If any of these men strove for everlasting remembrance, they must feel kinship with Nesselrode, who lived a diplomat, but is immortal as a pudding.[44]

What is wrong with perpetual charitable giving? At first glance, perpetual charitable giving appears to be ideal. After all, if charitable giving is good, isn't it even better for there to be more of it? Yet this analysis is based on two false premises: first, that giving in perpetuity creates more total charitable dollars than giving outright, and second, that people can address problems in the future as effectively as they can address problems in their own time. Both assumptions are questionable.

Many people undoubtedly choose to establish perpetual charitable trusts in the belief that more philanthropic dollars will ultimately be available by spending only income and preserving the principal in perpetuity. It is not surprising that people would assume that an infinite stream of payments (which is provided by setting aside principal and spending only income) will ultimately be greater than immediately spending the underlying income, and anyone familiar with the story of the goose that laid the golden eggs knows the importance of preserving principal. Fairy tales notwithstanding, however, this assumption of relative economic values does not necessarily hold true because it fails to consider the time value of money. The time value of money reflects the fact that because of lost earning capacity, a dollar one year from now is worth less than a dollar today. In many cases, setting principal aside and spending only income (even in perpetuity) produces less overall wealth than spending principal today.

Consider the example of a person with a million dollars to commit to charity. If it is spent immediately, then society gets the immediate full value of the one million dollars. What if instead the million is set aside in a private charitable foundation earning 5 percent each year and the foundation commits to spending all of its income on charitable endeavors (leaving aside the issue that it would likely need to spend a portion of that income on administration costs)? After how much time will the operating charities get the million dollars? One might initially calculate that it takes twenty years of fifty-thousand-dollar payments to equal one million dollars. Yet this fails to take into account the time value of money and the fact that each fifty-thousand-dollar payment is worth less in current dollars as each year passes. Thus, if fifty thousand dollars were to be paid one year from now (as opposed to today), and if the prevailing interest rates were 5 percent, then that fifty thousand one year from now would be worth only $47,619 in today's dollars. The fifty thousand distributed two years from now would be worth only $45,351 in today's dollars. How long would it take for the sum of these annual payments to equal a million dollars in today's dollars? Surprisingly, the answer is *never*. After a hundred years the sum of the present value of the annual payments is about $940,000, but owing to the diminished present value of payouts made far in the future, the next century of payments adds just ten thousand dollars in value in today's dollars, and no matter how far into the future one projects, the sum never equals the value of one million dollars today.

In addition to the limited economic value of perpetual charitable giving, there is another more deep-rooted problem. The perpetual charitable trust is founded on an assumption that people can make intelligent decisions about the use of resources in the distant future. It is not surprising that people would have this perception. The psychologist Daniel Gilbert has explained how humans are hardwired to make decisions on the assumption that the future is going to be essentially the same as the present (or, in the words of relief pitcher Dan Quisenberry, the future is the same as the present, only longer). Yet by looking back in time we can see how flawed this thinking is. Imagine the smartest person living five hundred years ago (Leonardo da Vinci, perhaps)—is there any question that no matter how extraordinarily smart that person was in his own time, his ability to make an intelligent allocation of resources in the twenty-first century would be extremely limited? Now extend that even farther back to a thousand or two thousand years ago. Does it really make sense for current policy to be dictated by plans established by someone living in the year 200? Yet that is precisely the situation that we are dictating for the future with perpetual charitable trusts.

Of course, this inquiry highlights the fundamental flaw of these perpetual entities. Namely, they are based on an assumption that the United States and its current system of laws will continue to exist in perpetuity. And yet in all of human history, few empires have lasted even a thousand years, let alone ten thousand or one hundred thousand.

Meanwhile, there are serious consequences to this system that encourages saving for tomorrow (and the next century and next millennium) instead of spending for today. Real problems are not being adequately addressed. Issues of environmental degradation, war and peace, hunger, infectious diseases, education, and multi-generational cycles of substance abuse and poverty are all problems in need of immediate resources. Yet in the pursuit of perpetuity, fewer resources are being devoted to these pressing issues.

Who benefits from this choice to direct charitable dollars to perpetual trusts instead of outright charitable gifts? The biggest beneficiaries are the trustees, who are paid large trustee salaries, and the supporting institutions, such as banks and other financial services companies, who are paid fees for managing this accumulating wealth.

Many people are surprised to learn that people often receive payment for serving on the boards of directors of private foundations (particularly in light of the hundreds of thousands of less well-off Americans who donate their time to serve on the boards of nonprofit organizations). These fees can be substantial—it is not uncommon for a trustee of a private foundation to be paid a hundred thousand dollars annually. A 2003 study analyzing tax returns of 238 private foundations revealed that in a single year, these organizations spent nearly $45 million on trustee fees—the bulk of which was paid to their own predominantly wealthy boards of directors. For some of these trusts, the money spent on trustee fees and other administrative expenses exceeded the amount spent on charitable endeavors.

Banks and financial service companies are the other beneficiaries. Assuming a modest 1 percent fee, the six hundred billion dollars currently in private foundations generates more than six billion dollars in management fees every year. Although perpetual charitable foundations may be a bad deal for society, they provide inordinate benefits to the financial services industry in the form of perpetual management fees.

Despite these problems, perpetual charitable organizations continue to be the preferred format for charitable giving. When people establish charitable foundations, they generally do so in perpetuity. In a 2004 survey of private foundations, only 9 percent of respondents said that their foundation would not exist in perpetuity.[45] This could be intentional on behalf of donors (an explicit desire to have their foundations address the problems of tomorrow as well as today), or perhaps it is because when they seek professional advice, the perpetual foundation is the one most likely to be presented to them. Regardless of the motivation, the results are undisputable: the vast majority of charitable foundations are established in perpetuity, and American law does nothing to discourage this.

Nonetheless, there has been some notable and powerful dissent against the tide of perpetuities. When billionaire investor Warren Buffet committed to contribute roughly thirty billion dollars to the largest private foundation in existence—the Bill and Melinda Gates Foundation—he did so on the condition that none of the donations be added to the principal and that all of Buffet's contributions be spent within one year of contribution.[46] Moreover, the Gates Foundation itself recently amended its charter to provide that it would end within fifty years after the death of the last of its trustees, Bill Gates, Melinda Gates, or Warren Buffet.

The law could be revised in a number of ways to make private foundations less focused on their perpetual existence and more responsive to societal needs. First, the law could require (as was proposed in 2003) that the 5 percent minimum payout rules must be satisfied with transfers to charity and not trustee fees and other administrative expenses. This would discourage private foundations from spending such a significant portion of their annual expenditures on administrative expenses. More directly the tax law could provide explicit limitations on the duration of private foundations or could provide that donors do not get their charitable deduction until the money is actually transferred for charitable purpose. Regardless of the method chosen, until the law takes a more concerted step to discourage perpetuities, we can expect more charitable dollars to be committed to perpetuating their own existence rather than toward their stated charitable goals.

Subsidized Charitable Giving

For most of history, charitable giving has occurred independent of any government support. However, for the past century charitable donations (both while living and at death) in the United States have been subsidized by the government through the charitable deduction.

During life, this subsidy is limited; the charitable deduction is available to offset only approximately half of a person's taxable income. Charitable transfers at death, however, are under no such limitation. Any individual, no matter how wealthy, can avoid all estate taxes by taking advantage of the unlimited charitable deduction. In 2007 the hotel real estate magnate Leona Helmsley effectively eliminated the estate tax liability on her five-billion-plus-dollar estate by transferring the bulk of her assets to the Harry and Leona Helmsley Charitable Trust.

People often think of government expenditures solely in terms of direct monetary outlays by the government for particular programs, such as national defense, Medicaid, and Medicare. Yet it has long been recognized that another way the government spends its resources is through the tax system.[47] Some tax deductions (as well as exclusions and credits) can be the equivalent of direct government expenditures and are termed "tax expenditures." As explained by the Senate Budget Committee in the 1970s: "Tax expenditures are revenue losses that occur as a result of Federal tax provisions that grant special relief to encourage certain kinds of activities by taxpayers or to aid taxpayers in special circumstances. The net result of these provisions is equivalent to the simultaneous collection of revenue and a direct budget outlay of an equal amount."[48]

When the government grants tax benefits for money spent purchasing a fuel-efficient car, it is the same as if the government were assisting the purchaser of the car by contributing to the cost of the purchase price. Similarly, tax expenditure analysis enables the home mortgage deduction to be appropriately analyzed for what it is: a federal grant to people who take out loans to purchase a home that is not available to people who rent or to people who own their homes outright.

In the context of charity, tax expenditures operate like matching grants.

As one scholar explains: "The charitable deduction makes the government a partner in every gift-giving venture; a taxpayer in the (hypothetical, but arithmetically convenient) 50 percent bracket, for instance, can be seen as joining forces with the government to give equal amounts to the cause chosen by the taxpayer (with characteristics or minimum qualifications set by the government)."[49]

When a taxpayer who would otherwise be subject to a 45 percent tax rate makes a deductible transfer of a hundred dollars to the American Red Cross and gets a reduction in his or her taxes of forty-five dollars, it is the same as if the taxpayer were contributing fifty-five dollars to the Red Cross and directing the government to make a matching grant of forty-five dollars to the Red Cross.

The charitable deduction is a particularly costly expenditure. The *New York Times* reported in 2007 that "the charitable deduction cost the government $40 billion in lost tax revenue last year, according to the Joint Committee on Taxation, more than the government spends altogether on managing public lands, protecting the environment and developing new energy sources."[50]

Legal scholar Saul Levmore supports the charitable deduction as an efficient way for the government to get information from the populace regarding which programs it ought to support. He analogizes the charitable deduction to the taxpayer checkoff regarding financing elections but regards the charitable deduction as superior because it is likely to reflect a more thoughtful choice since it requires the donor to make a cash outlay.

Although the charitable deduction does give the government information about how some taxpayers would like to direct governmental resources, there are nonetheless serious policy concerns with using this as a directive for governmental expenditures, particularly in the estate tax context.

Most significantly, the matching grant program is only available to the charitable donations of the very wealthy. For income tax purposes, it applies only to those who itemize their deductions, and for gift and estate tax purposes, it applies only to individuals with estates that are larger than $3.5 million. Thus, if a person with a multimillion-dollar estate, subject to a 45 percent tax, makes a one-hundred-thousand-dollar charitable donation, that donation is functionally equivalent to the donor making a fifty-five-thousand-dollar donation and the federal government making a forty-five-thousand-dollar donation to the charity chosen by the wealthy donor. However, if that same hundred-thousand-dollar donation is made by someone who is not otherwise subject to the estate tax (because his or her estate is less than \$3.5 million in 2009), then the charitable bequest offers no financial benefit to the donor's estate, and there is no functional federal contribution to the donor's chosen charity. In this way, the matching grant program is highly distorted because it considers only the preferences of the wealthiest Americans.

This matching grant for the preferences of the wealthy is particularly troubling because wealthy Americans tend to make very different types of bequests than their fellow citizens. Whereas most Americans direct their charitable dollars to religious organizations, approximately three-fourths of all bequests reported on estate tax returns go to either private foundations or educational institutions.[51] This type of giving by the wealthy raises the question of whether the charitable deduction is the most efficient use of taxpayer dollars because charitable gifts to private foundations and educational institutions both raise policy concerns.

Private foundations receive almost half of all charitable bequests. As discussed above, private foundations are a form of charitable trusts that do not generally engage in charitable work themselves but instead dispense a portion of their assets each year to support the work of other charitable organizations. The vast majority of private foundations are designed to exist in perpetuity and therefore only spend a small portion of their asset value each year on charitable endeavors. Thus, although a taxpayer who transfers a million dollars to his or her charitable foundation will get an up-front deduction worth \$450,000 (effectively a \$450,000 matching grant from the federal government), the foundation will only be required to spend about fifty thousand dollars each year. Since this fifty thousand is just as likely to be spent on administrative expenses as it is on charitable grants, this further lessens the likelihood that charities will ever receive the full benefit of the million dollars.

The second largest group of recipients of beneficence from wealthy individuals is educational institutions. Although education plays an important role for all sectors of society, the allocation of resources by the wealthy raises other issues. Rather than distributing this wealth broadly, a disproportionate share of these bequests goes to a small number of selective, socially prestigious schools. Legal scholar Miranda Perry calculates that twenty-five private colleges and universities (out of almost seventeen hundred private colleges and universities) and ten socially prestigious private schools (out of more than twenty-seven thousand such institutions) received approximately 23 percent of all education bequests reported on 2005 estate tax returns.[52] It is unlikely that the population as a whole would support federal matching grants for Exeter Academy while so many public schools are failing to meet the needs of the larger population. Political scientist Rob Reich has argued that this type of educational philanthropy can actually impose a societal detriment by increasing the gap between the wealthy and the poor, particularly in the context of education.[53]

Finally, even when charitable dollars are oriented toward the truly needy it is still questionable whether it is in society's interest to allow private individuals to effectively direct so many federal resources toward their chosen causes. The Gates Foundation has given a significant amount of its grants to improve the lives of the poor in developing countries. Although this is important work, the effect of the charitable deduction is that the American public has effectively underwritten several billion dollars' worth of foreign aid by private individuals—even though polls show Americans are ambivalent about using tax dollars for such assistance.[54]

Transfers for Other Purposes

In the preceding section we explored how transfers for charitable purposes are supported and encouraged in the law. Not only are people allowed to make transfers for charitable purposes, but beyond that the law supports the implementation of people's charitable plans in perpetuity, and the wealthiest Americans have their charitable bequests subsidized by the government through the charitable deduction.

What about transfers for purposes other than those that are considered charitable? Some of the common noncharitable purposes that people seek to fulfill are the care of a pet, the maintenance of a grave, or the publication (or destruction) of personal papers. Does the law respect such requests? Here the law is far less generous. These transfers for noncharitable purposes are at best tolerated in limited circumstances, but just as often they are disallowed.

Sometimes people want to spend money for certain purposes that are neither charitable nor considered against public policy. Some of the more common goals that people want to accomplish are maintaining a gravesite, building a monument, or caring for a pet. During life, these purposes are easily accomplished: people regularly hire others to perform these services, and if the person hired fails to perform these services in a satisfactory manner, the person simply hires someone else. However, after death people are dependent on the law to ensure that their wishes are carried out. To what extent can someone continue to exert influence on the world by leaving money to be used to accomplish a noncharitable purpose?

As discussed in chapter 2, the legal mechanism for leaving instructions with respect to the use of property is the trust. At first glance it might appear that a trust is the perfect vehicle for accomplishing these goals. Yet there is a practical problem with the use of trusts for noncharitable purposes: how to ensure that the money is spent in accordance with the settlor's wishes. Trusts that are established for the benefit of individuals can be enforced by the individual beneficiary. Trusts that are established for charitable purposes can be enforced by the state attorney general, who is both authorized and obligated to enforce charitable trusts. But when a person tries to establish a trust for the benefit of a dog or for the building of a monument, who will ensure that the trustee does what he or she is supposed to do? A dog cannot enforce a trust for its own benefit, and the attorney general has no obligation to enforce trusts that do not serve the public benefit. For this reason, trusts for noncharitable purposes were not recognized in nineteenth-century America and are still not recognized today in England. The effect of this rule is that if someone left money for a particular noncharitable purpose (such as the care of a dog or a grave), the trust could not be fulfilled even if the named trustee was willing to do so. However, in the early twentieth century, American law broke from English law by explicitly recognizing certain types of noncharitable purpose trusts.

The 1935 Restatement of Law provided that when property is transferred for a specific noncharitable purpose, although it will not be treated as a trust (since there is no beneficiary to enforce it), the person receiving the property has the option to apply the property to the designated purpose or surrender it to the estate (in which case the bequest would fail). This provision for the first time allowed noncharitable trusts to be fulfilled, provided that the time period for the trust was limited by the Rule against Perpetuities.[55] These trusts have come to be called "honorary trusts." The term is a misnomer, however, because they really aren't trusts at all.

Honorary trusts are recognized throughout the United States today. However, they do not provide the same assurances as private trusts and charitable trusts that their settlor's wishes will be carried out. Thus, although Leona Helmsley provided in her will that twelve million dollars should be set aside for the care of her dog, the court later reduced that amount to a mere two million.[56]

Capricious Purpose

Although people are allowed to spend at whim during life, the law applies its own limiting standards for transfers at death. The stated reason for this is that bequests for capricious purposes need to be curtailed because unlike lifetime consumption, they are uninhibited by the restraint of self-interest. As one scholar puts it: "However much the dead possess, it too is more than they can spend; hence they can squander it with abandon."[57] Because of this concern that people are more likely to make inappropriate choices at death than they are during life (since they won't have to suffer the consequences of a bad choice), the law provides that if property is transferred to someone to fulfill a capricious purpose, no trust is created and the person has no power to apply the property to that purpose. Moreover, if the individual does so, he or she is liable to the estate. This provides an incentive for someone in receipt of property to get court approval before following the directions laid out by a decedent if there is a chance the purpose will be found to be capricious.

It is not always easy to determine what constitutes a "capricious" purpose. Indeed, the Restatement of Trust Law, the compilation and analysis of law prepared by the American Law Institute, acknowledges that it is not just difficult but impossible to draw a clear line between purposes that are capricious and those that are not. The use of the word "capricious" (which means impulsive or unpredictable) suggests that the determination is made by considering the level of care taken by the donor in his decision-making. The Restatement of Trust law seems to support this subjective standard when it states that "a purpose is not capricious merely because no living person benefits from its performance." However, the next phrase belies this subjective standard by stating: all that matters is that "it satisfies a *natural* desire which *normal* people have with respect to the disposition of their property."[58] Use of the terms "natural" and "normal" reveal that the applicable standard is determined by reference to objective social values (or more accurately the subjective values of the judge rendering the decision regarding what is socially valuable) rather than the thoughtfulness of the person making the bequest.

Case law in the area suggests that courts are indeed applying their own standards of appropriateness. Thus courts have invalidated trusts for the purpose of turning a person's house into a museum and for the publication of a person's writing or scientific theories that the court viewed to be without merit.

This last category has proved to be most affected by the idiosyncrasies of the judge ruling on the case as courts are often asked to consider whether the publication promotes a public benefit (and therefore qualifies as charitable, with all of its benefits under the law) or whether the purpose is capricious, and therefore against public policy. This tension was evidenced in a 1982 case involving the will of a woman who sought to establish a trust for publication of her book *Linda* about her daughter, who had died at a young age from cancer. The lower court ruled that the trust did not have a charitable purpose since the book had "no literary value" and its dissemination would produce "no public benefit." On appeal, although the court received evidence that the book was "ungodly bad," it nonetheless ruled that publication of the book was "charitable" regardless of the work's literary merit.[59]

In a similar case—with drastically different results—Theodore Schroeder sought to use his estate to publish his writings after death. Schroeder was a lawyer who retired in 1904 to devote himself to writing. In 1911 he privately published a book, *Obscene Literature and Constitutional Law*, which argued for the abolition of laws against obscene language.

Schroeder was a prolific writer and wrote hundreds of articles on many issues. The articles were frequently critical of religious practice in general and the Mormon Church in particular. Schroeder considered himself a "controversialist," and many of his articles bore provocative titles, such as "Divinity in Semen," "Shaker Celibacy and Salacity," "Phallic Worship to Secularized Sex," "Mormonism and Prostitution," and "Was Joseph Smith, 'The Prophet,' an 'Abortionist'?" At his death in 1953, Schroeder left a will that gave his entire estate in trust for the "collection and arrangement and publication of [his] writing."

In determining whether this constituted a valid charitable purpose, the Connecticut Supreme Court began by acknowledging that a trust to promote dissemination of a person's writings is normally considered to be charitable, regardless of the literary merit of the writing. But the court went on to provide as follows: "The law will not declare a trust valid when the object of the trust, as the finding discloses, is to distribute articles which reek of the sewer. The very enumeration of some of the titles which Schroeder selected for his writings brands them indelibly and a reading of the article which he called 'Prenatal Psychisms and Mystical Pantheism' is a truly nauseating experience in the field of pornography. The trust is invalid as being contrary to public policy."[60]

The court in *Schroeder* ruled that the purpose of the trust was so abhorrent that it was not only invalid as a charitable trust, but it was also not a valid private trust because it was against public policy. As a result, the court ruled that the money that would have been spent on publication of Schroeder's work would instead pass to his heirs—two first cousins in whom the court noted the decedent had "no interest."

Despite the court's assessment of Schroeder's writings, history has evaluated them differently. Schroeder's book and other essays—decried by the court as "reeking of the sewer"—have been reprinted numerous times in the half century since his death. Indeed, *Obscene Literature and Constitutional Law* has been reissued several times, most recently in 2002. Moreover, Schroeder's personal papers are currently held in the Rare Books and Manuscript Division of the New York Public Library.

The law regarding trusts for a purpose has been most consistent when it comes to the issue of bequests that provide for the destruction of property. The Restatement of Trust law states that "it is capricious to provide that money shall be thrown into the sea or that a field shall be sowed with salt or that a house shall be boarded up and remain unoccupied."[61] Even though a person would be allowed to do any of these things during life with his or her own property, the individual could not direct someone else to do it after his or her death; and if that someone else did carry out those wishes, he or she would be liable to the estate for the economic loss from the destruction.

At first glance, ordering the destruction of property appears to be the clearest example of the type of instruction that can only be made capriciously (impulsively and with little forethought); however, there are many reasons why a *normal* person would have a *natural* desire to destroy property. For example, many people keep private letters and diaries during their lives but would not like to have them revealed to others after death. In that case it is quite natural for a normal person to request that these papers be destroyed. Jacqueline Susann, best-selling author of *Valley of the Dolls*, asked her executor to destroy her diary "so that its contents would never become public and embarrass those mentioned within it."[62] In a similar case (but one that was not subject to legal challenge), Jacqueline Kennedy Onassis gave her personal papers to her children and requested that they take whatever action was warranted in order to respect her wish for privacy by preventing "the display, publication or distribution, in whole or in part, of these papers, letters and writings."

In another example, consider the case of an artist who produced some works that did not meet his personal standards (perhaps they were produced late in life as his capacity waned). In order to protect his reputation, as well as the value of his other works, the artist might want to have these substandard works destroyed at his death. This desire to destroy creative work that the artist perceives is substandard has a long history. The cases that are best known to us, however, are ones where this wish was not carried out. In 10 BC, Virgil wrote a will that contained a provision requesting that his executor burn the *Aeneid*. Similarly, Franz Kafka directed his executor, Max Brod, to destroy all of his unpublished written works, including the sole copies of his two then-unpublished masterpieces, *The Castle* and *The Trial*. Although neither wish was carried out, Virgil's and Kafka's desires were not necessarily capricious.

In many other countries, the right of an artist to destroy his or her work is explicitly protected under moral rights (called "droit morale"). Moral rights are based on the notion that an artist's identity is closely tied to his or her artistic creations, and as such the artist has an interest in which creations are made public and which are destroyed. Moral rights are discussed in greater detail in the next chapter. Here, however, it is important to note that moral rights survive the artist's death and that requests for posthumous control are much more likely to be requested.

American law does not look favorably on the destruction of property, regardless of how understandable the person's desires might be. The law limits this type of destruction in two ways. First, the law provides that if property is transferred to someone to fulfill a capricious purpose, no trust is created and the person has no power to apply the property to that purpose. Moreover, if the person does, he or she is liable to the estate for doing so. This provides an incentive for a person in receipt of property to get court approval before following the directions laid out by a decedent if there is a chance that the purpose will be found to be capricious.

In addition to disallowing the destruction of this type of property, the law deters this type of destruction by imposing an estate tax on the full market value of the property—even if the testator has ordered the property destroyed. Thus, although Jacqueline Susann's executor did in fact destroy her diaries, the Internal Revenue Service valued the diary at $3.8 million and taxed the estate accordingly.[63] This imposition of estate taxes can create a significant estate tax liability, and in some cases the need to raise money to cover the estate tax liability can result in the executor's inability to carry out the decedent's wishes. There is also a certain irony in that the people who are most mindful of their privacy are likely to suffer the greatest estate tax liability because of the market appeal of highly personal letters of a private person.

4

CONTROLLING REPUTATION

How will we be remembered after we are gone? This is primarily an extralegal question; its answer lies largely outside the realm of the law and resides in a combination of our lifetime actions with the values and interests of those who knew us, as well as, perhaps even more important, the values of subsequent generations. The poet Shelley captured the fleeting nature of power and fame in "Ozymandias"—once a "king of kings" but now merely a crumbling statue in the desert.

History is replete with tales of people—think of the author Herman Melville and the artist Vincent Van Gogh—who died in obscurity only to be subsequently revered. And many people who were famous and well regarded in their own time have since fallen into the dustbin of history. Consider the case of Frances Willard. Although her statue is on display in Statutory Hall in Washington, DC, as the most honored citizen of Illinois, few people today could tell you who she was. During her life, Willard was a leading advocate of women's rights and a leader in the temperance movement. She was as well known to Americans in her time as Eleanor Roosevelt would be half a century later. At her death in 1898, Willard was one of the most famous women in America. Flags flew at half-mast in New York, Washington, and Chicago, and thirty thousand mourners passed by her casket in one day. One New York newspaper wrote: "No woman's name is better known in the English speaking world then that of Miss Willard, save that of England's great queen." Another declared that she was the most influential woman of the age and that her name would become more and more revered in ages to come. This was not to pass, however. Although her name lives on as the namesake of several elementary schools and a college dormitory, it has otherwise been largely eclipsed by contemporaries who were less well known in their lifetime, such as Elizabeth Cady Stanton and Susan B. Anthony. Some have suggested that Willard's fall from fame was due to her work on behalf of the temperance movement—a cause later generations repudiated.[1]

Changes in reputation can be caused by events entirely outside of an individual's control. Clyde William Tombaugh was an astronomer made famous by his discovery of the ninth planet, Pluto, in 1930. As the only person in the western hemisphere to have discovered a planet, Tombaugh could have justifiably believed that his reputation was secured when he died at the age of ninety in 1997. Less than ten years after his death, however, Pluto was stripped of its planetary status, and Tombaugh's reputation was likely diminished, too.

Although it may not be defining in terms of a person's posthumous reputation, the law nonetheless plays an important role in allowing or restricting the flow of information about a person, which can in turn affect his or her reputation. Consider the varying likely effects of the following possible stances that the law could take regarding reputations of the dead. At one extreme, the law could prohibit any actions that blackened the memory of the dead. These prohibitions could be enforced either by a person's heirs or by a governmental agency or prosecutor. At the other extreme, the law could lift all restrictions at death, and everything about a person could fall into the public domain, including his or her name, image, creative works, privacy, and secrets.

Reputation and the Law

Even more than one's body or property, one's reputation is often essential. As Cassio says in Shakespeare's *Othello:* "Reputation, reputation, reputation! O, I have lost my reputation. I have lost the immortal part of myself, and what remains is bestial."[2]

Reputation is hard to control because it is the byproduct of wide-ranging information. Nonetheless, the law uses four essential doctrines to protect a person's reputation: the law of defamation, including libel and slander, which provides protection against written and spoken falsehoods that harm a person's reputation; the right of privacy, which allows people to protect themselves against unwelcome publicity regarding their private affairs; the right of publicity, which allows people to control the commercial exploitation of their name, likeness, or personality; and copyright law, which provides protections for a person's creative expressions. Together these provisions create a protective web, giving Americans a significant degree of control over their reputations during life.

What about after death? Here American law develops a distinctly split personality. The areas of law most directly concerned with reputation—defamation and privacy—strictly adhere to the position that a person has no interest in his or her reputation after death. Where reputational interests blend with or have been converted into property interests, however, the law has moved to granting greater rights to the dead, regardless of the costs imposed on the living.

Defamation

Texas attorney Barr McClellan had a theory that former vice president Lyndon B. Johnson was involved in both the planning and later cover-up of the assassination of former president John F. Kennedy. In 2003 he wrote a best-selling book that stated so explicitly. In the following year he repeated the charges in a documentary that aired on the History Channel.[3]

Famous and powerful people were outraged by the decision of the History Channel to broadcast this program to its 125 million subscribers. Former presidents Jimmy Carter and Gerald Ford, along with Lady Bird Johnson and journalist Bill Moyers, expressed indignation that such outlandish and damaging accusations could be presented in such a one-sided way. As former president Carter said: "If it can happen to him, it could happen to me after I'm dead."[4] What made the critics so angry was that none of the people accused were alive to defend themselves. Of course, if the people had been living, none of these accusations would likely have been made for fear of incurring a defamation lawsuit. However, because a dead person cannot be defamed, Barr McClellan, as well as his publisher and the History Channel, could act with impunity.

The law of defamation (the umbrella term for the legal claims of libel and slander) protects living people's reputations against false and derogatory comments.[5] Defamation as a cause of action has a long pedigree: it originated in the common law of sixteenth-century England and has existed in the United States since the nation's inception. Defamation generally protects individuals against the publication of false statements that harm their reputation. The only limitation on claims for defamation during life is that if the person making the claim is a public official, then he or she must prove that the person publishing the falsehood did so either knowingly or recklessly.[6] A person who has been defamed is entitled to recover for all harms caused by injury to his or her reputation. Thus, a collector of antique tools who got into a dispute over a trade with another collector was entitled to recover for defamation when the other person created a web page to warn others against dealing with him. The posting accused the trader of being a "flat-out liar and cheat" and a "drunk" who is "in the denial stages of his problem." The jury awarded the plaintiff $150,000 for his defamation claim.[7]

After death the picture is quite different. Here the law does a radical about-face and provides essentially no protection against defamation. The reason most commonly given for this rule is that a dead person is beyond harm or benefit. As one court described it: "Once a person is dead, there is no extant reputation to injure or for the law to protect."[8] This principle is illustrated in a recent case when a husband and wife were murdered by one of their six children. As if the story was not lurid enough, the television station reporting the story added the following tidbit: "In an odd twist to this story, sources close to the investigation say that David Johnson, Sr. and his wife Ruby were also twins, brother and sister." This rather remarkable fact of twin siblings marrying each other and giving birth to six children was completely false, and the television station was promptly informed of this. Nonetheless, the station continued to report the story and refused to issue a retraction. The other children of the murder victims brought a defamation suit against the television station on behalf of their deceased parents. However, the court ruled that no claim could be brought on behalf of the parents because their reputation no longer existed after death, and therefore it couldn't be harmed.[9]

What about family members or other loved ones? Surely they suffer when falsehoods are published about those they love who are no longer living. Nonetheless, the law is clear that family members also cannot sue for defamation of their loved ones (whether alive or dead). Thus in the above case, the court ruled not only that was there no claim on behalf of the parents but that there was also no claim on behalf of the children because the harm was personal to the parents.[10]

The lack of legal protections for interests of the dead encourages the spreading of highly sensational material since this tends to be most profitable for publishers. However, since the public is generally not aware of the lack of protection for the dead, they may assume that the publishers have the same incentives for veracity that they do when publishing information about living people. Because it permits inaccuracies and untruths to flourish, the prevalence of such journalism can have negative social consequences.

State legislatures periodically have taken up proposals that would allow defamation claims to survive death, but these proposals have been largely unsuccessful. Thus, the New York legislature considered adopting a statute that would have created a new cause of action for defamation of the dead and would have allowed family members to bring a defamation claim within five years of a person's death. Although it was considered in a variety of forms over multiple years, the legislation never passed.[11] To date, the only state to enact any protections against defamation of the dead is Rhode Island. However, the Rhode Island protections are extremely limited—applying only to defamatory remarks made in an obituary within three months of a person's death.

Right of Privacy

People's reputations during life are also protected by the right of privacy. However, like the law of defamation, the right of privacy does not extend its protection to people who are no longer living.

Most tort claims, like claims for defamation, originated from the common law of England. The right of privacy is unusual in that it is of fairly recent vintage—dating to the early twentieth century—and rather than coming from the courts of England was instead native to the United States, originating from an 1890 law review article called "The Right of Privacy" that was written by Samuel Warren and Louis Brandeis (later Supreme Court justice).[12] In that article Warren and Brandeis urged courts to recognize the development of a common law right to privacy. This right "to be let alone"[13] was designed to secure individuals' ability to protect their solitude by controlling the public use of their name or likeness.[14] According to the authors, the need for recognition of this right stemmed from changes in technology and business methods, which made this additional protection necessary: "Instantaneous photographs and newspaper enterprise have invaded the sacred precincts of private and domestic life; and numerous mechanical devices threaten to make good the prediction that what is whispered in the closet shall be proclaimed from the house-tops."[15] The right to privacy was thus fashioned as a right to maintain human dignity in an increasingly undignified world.[16]

The right to privacy first enunciated by Warren and Brandeis was subsequently recognized explicitly in every state, either by common law or statute.[17] In practice, however, it has provided far less protection than early proponents had hoped because it has been curtailed by the constitutional protections afforded free speech, particularly by the press. Within this protection, anything that is deemed "newsworthy" (tending to cover anything that a newspaper is interested in publishing) is not protected by the right of privacy.[18] This has caused one scholar to refer to the right of privacy as a "phantom tort" that generates false hopes for plaintiffs.[19]

The area where privacy protection tends to be more robust in American law is when it is protecting against government intrusion into people's lives. Accordingly, laws interfering with people's choices about sexual partners and the use of contraceptives have been found to violate their right to privacy. In addition, outside the context of the press, the right to privacy does provide some protections against dissemination of private information. Thus, a successful privacy case was brought by a person whose name was displayed on a large poster carried by a protester outside an abortion clinic.[20]

However limited the protections of privacy are during life, they are completely absent after death. It is a settled principle of American law that the right of privacy (like the claim for defamation) does not continue after death. Thus, one leading treatise describes the rights of the dead in this area as follows: "The law allows scholars, pop history writers and gossip magazines to roar away about the dead: they are beyond caring.

If offspring and relatives are upset, their remedy is to respond with the truth."[21]

The reason for this failure to protect reputational interests of the dead is both theoretical and practical. The theory of privacy law is that it protects against feelings of embarrassment. American law takes the position that since a dead person cannot be embarrassed, he or she cannot suffer the harm protected by defamation or invasion of privacy. The failure to protect reputational interests also effectively avoids a more practical problem: If a right to privacy was found to exist for dead people, how could the claim be asserted? American law lacks a mechanism through which a dead person's reputational interest can be exercised. A dead person's wishes with respect to his or her property are protected through the legal system of probate, which appoints a representative of the decedent's wishes for the limited time necessary to distribute the estate. But if there was posthumous legal protection for reputation, there would need to be a mechanism through which that person's interest could be represented for so long as the right existed. Since there is no such mechanism under current American law, it makes practical sense that this interest is not protected.

Despite this fixed common law rule that the right to privacy does not survive death, in recent years there has been a small chink in the armor. That is in connection with the government's releasing information to the public under the Freedom of Information Act (FOIA) and similar state statutes governing the release of information by the government to the public. FOIA was enacted in the wake of the Watergate scandal in order to facilitate public access to government documents. FOIA contains a privacy exception that allows the government to not disclose those items that might violate a person's right to privacy. This exception enables the government to keep individual tax returns, as well as other material considered to be private, from being released to the public at large. Generally speaking, the privacy exception in FOIA does not protect interests of people who are no longer living. In 2004, however, the Supreme Court considered the application of that privacy exception to death-scene photographs of the body of Vince Foster, President Bill Clinton's deputy counsel, after Foster purportedly committed suicide.[22] The Court ruled that although Foster himself no longer had a right of privacy (because he was dead), his family was entitled to use the privacy protections of FOIA to keep the images from being divulged. In making this ruling, the Court made clear that it was protecting not the dead per se but the interests of the living:

> It is the right of privacy of the living which it is sought to enforce here. That right may in some cases be itself violated by improperly interfering with the character or memory of a deceased relative, but it is the right of the living, and not that of the dead, which is recognized. A privilege may be given the surviving relatives of a deceased person to protect his memory, but the privilege exists for the benefit of the living, to protect their feelings, and to prevent a violation of their own rights in the character and memory of the deceased.[23]

A similar analysis was used to protect against disclosure of tapes of 911 emergency calls made by dying victims of a nightclub fire[24] as well as the dying words of callers made to 911 emergency operators on 11 September 2001 from the World Trade Center towers.[25]

Although these cases may seem to extend privacy protections to family members, it is important to note that they do not provide a general relational right of privacy but rather merely limit public access to government information and documents. Courts continue to refuse to recognize general privacy claims brought by relatives in relation to the dead. This difference was highlighted in a California case where the court dismissed an action brought by the family of a man whose body was photographed at the scene of his murder in a public park. The picture appeared in the newspaper as part of the year-end news summary. The family complained, and although the newspaper issued an apology, the court refused to find any liability, explicitly drawing a distinction between the line of cases arising from FOIA and the common law claim for invasion of right of privacy. With respect to the latter, the court stated: "It is well settled that the right of privacy is purely a personal one; it cannot be asserted by anyone other than the person whose privacy has been invaded, that is, plaintiff must plead and prove that his privacy has been invaded. . . . Further, the right does not survive but dies with the person."[26]

The reasoning behind the refusal of American law to extend protection to reputations of the dead is often couched in terms of logic: after death there is no reputation to be harmed nor for the law to protect. In this way, harm to reputation is treated like pain and suffering—something that obviously does not apply to the dead. The simplicity of this statement belies the complexity of the issue of posthumous harm, however, and in particular the question of whether a person can be harmed by assaults on his or her reputation after death. This question has puzzled philosophers for centuries.[27] It should not surprise us, therefore, that different societies have taken different positions with respect to this issue. Whereas American law provides almost no protection for reputations of the dead, European law has taken a very different approach. In general, continental European countries provide extensive protections for an individual's reputation, even after death. A comparison of Italian law with American law illustrates several critical differences.

The first area where Italian law stands in stark contrast with American law is in enforcement. One issue that is inherent in any system that seeks to protect interests of the dead is what mechanism is available for enforcement. One of the limitations of American law is that there is no individual or entity charged with representing the privacy interests of deceased individuals. For distribution of property, American law has an elaborate system of executors, trustees, and other individuals charged with representing the decedent's wishes. For property committed to charitable purpose, the state attorney general is charged with representing the decedent's interests. Yet when it comes to reputational interests, there is no individual or governmental entity charged with protecting the deceased individual's reputation under American law. In contrast, Italian law addresses this problem by establishing a governmental agency whose purpose is to protect individuals' privacy. This agency is known as the Authority for the Protection of Privacy (Garante per la protezione dei dati personali).

This agency has issued a number of rulings that give the flavor of the extent of the Italian protections of the dead. A classic example of a case protected under Italian law involved a man named Franco Scoglio who died during the filming of a television show. The Authority for the Protection of Privacy issued a press release that stated that the television images could not be displayed because it would be a violation of Scoglio's right to privacy. Scoglio had a right to have the moment of his death not displayed before the public.[28]

The privacy protections under Italian law are not limited to individuals who generally live outside the public eye. Thus, when Saddam Hussein was executed in December 2006, the authority issued a press release to the media directing them to be careful of how they showed the events. They were ordered to be careful to protect the dignity of the person.[29]

Finally, the Italian magazine *Chi* purchased the worldwide exclusive right to publish pictures of Lady Diana that were taken at the moment after her fatal accident when the emergency medical technicians had just arrived at the scene of the accident. The editors also acquired the findings of the autopsy that was performed on her body. The court ruled ex officio that it was a violation of Princess Diana's personal dignity to disclose any of this information and that such disclosure was not justified under any need for free information to the public. It also ruled that any further dissemination of this information would be forbidden and that anyone violating the order could be subject to criminal sanctions, including a prison sentence of up to two years.[30]

Italian law is particularly protective of the interests of minors. When a teenage boy committed suicide in Italy, a newspaper published pictures of the boy's house as well as the text of an essay he had written on the day of his suicide. The boy's father asked that the newspaper stop publication of these things and sought damages for past publication. The agency ruled that the privacy of minors after death is subject to special consideration. It awarded damages and ordered that the magazine had to stop publishing pictures of the house as well as excerpts from the boy's essay. The agency also ordered an investigation into how the reporter got the essay.[31]

This case stands in sharp contrast to a similar case from the United States involving a teen suicide. In the American case, police officers took photographs of the sixteen-year-old as he lay in his coffin and subse-

quently displayed the photographs at a public gathering. There the officers made statements that the boy's involvement in gang-related activities had caused his death. The boy's mother sued for invasion of privacy.
The court, in rejecting her claim, ruled that there was no cause of action
for invasion of privacy on behalf of the boy because he was dead and no
cause of action on behalf of the mother because any claim of right to privacy was personal to the son.[32]

Italy is not alone in providing postmortem protection for a person's
reputation. The "right of personality" has been recognized in the German constitution since 1954. This section guarantees protection of every
person's human dignity and right to free development of personality.[33]
The protection of human dignity has been found to continue, even after
death, by the German constitutional court in a famous case referred to as
the *Mephisto* case.[34] *Mephisto* involved a novel of the same name written
by Klaus Mann (son of Thomas Mann) in 1936 after he was forced to
leave Germany. One of the fictional characters in his novel was based on
the life of German actor and theater director Gustav Gründgens, who
had cooperated with the Nazis to advance his artistic career. When the
novel was about to be published in West Germany in 1963, both Mann
and Gründgens were dead. Nonetheless, Gründgens's adoptive son (and
sole heir) successfully sued the publisher to prevent publication of the
novel on the grounds that it would violate the honor, reputation, and
memory of Gründgens. In siding with Gründgens's son, the court ruled
that an individual's death does not put an end to the obligation of a
country to protect that individual against violation of his or her human
dignity. The court also ruled that there was no set period for this right of
dignity, and it could survive longer than thirty years after the person's
death. The *Mephisto* decision had limited practical effect because the book
had already been published in East Germany and was readily available to
the West. Although *Mephisto* was eventually published in West Germany
in 1980 (by a different publisher), the case highlights some of the costs of
having the right of privacy survive death. In particular, the ability to write
biography, history, and even fiction can be inhibited by this type of protection.

What explains this different treatment of privacy such that American law sees no violation where Italian and German law does? James Whitman has noted that although European countries and the United States all provide protections for "privacy," the notions of what constitutes a violation of privacy are very different. American law is primarily concerned with privacy as a mode of protecting individual liberty—particularly from governmental intrusion—whereas European law views privacy as a way to protect human dignity, particularly from being degraded by the press. In this way, European law comes much closer to capturing the concerns originally set out by Warren and Brandeis in their seminal article, which gave birth to American privacy law.

European privacy law stems from the extensive set of rules available to the aristocratic classes in the nineteenth century to allow them to protect their reputations. The effect of the greater equalization that occurred over the twentieth century was that protections for reputational interests, previously applicable only to the aristocracy, became available to everyone. Whitman refers to this phenomenon as "equaling down" and describes it as follows: "After many generations of experience, Europeans have come to value a certain kind of personhood: a kind of personhood founded in the commitment to a society in which every person, of every social station, has the right to put on a respectable public face; a society in which privacy rights are not just for royalty, but for *everybody*."[35]

Ironically, it may have been the early attempts to erase class distinctions in the United States that has resulted today in so few protections for the reputations of the average American.

Right of Publicity and Copyright

Every year *Forbes* magazine publishes its list of "Top-Earning Dead Celebrities." As the editors explained in the 2006 edition, "A nail in the casket is hardly the end for some stars. Instead, their work, as well as their iconic images, continues to appeal to fans who remember them, and to those born long after they died." Top earners that year included the musicians Kurt Cobain, Elvis Presley, John Lennon, Ray Charles, and Johnny Cash, whose music has continued to sell, as well as such writers and artists as Charles M. Schulz, J. R. R. Tolkien, and Theodor Geisel, better known as Dr. Seuss, whose written works have also remained popular. However, the list also included such names as Marilyn Monroe and Albert Einstein, who have had lucrative posthumous careers not because of continued sales of their work but rather through the marketing of their name and image.

More recently, a new record has been set for posthumous money-making. In the seven weeks after his death, Michael Jackson's estate reportedly earned one hundred million dollars (from, among other things, a film deal, a commemorative coin, a line of school supplies, and a $150 coffee-table book), and it was expected to earn another hundred million by the end of 2009. The value of Jackson's intellectual property rights was estimated to be worth at least in the hundreds of millions of dollars.[36]

Of course, in order for the continued interest by the public in these dead celebrities to translate into dollars, the law must provide a mechanism that allows some, but not others, to control the exploitation. For example, although Shakespeare plays may be steady sellers and his image iconic, Shakespeare is not a top earner: people do not need to pay to reproduce his works or image because both belong to the public domain.

The two legal rights that generally make it possible for celebrities to continue to generate revenue after death are the right of publicity, which allows a person to control the exploitation of his or her image, and copyright law, which allows a person to control the exploitation of his or her creations. Unlike the protections provided by defamation and right of privacy, which under American law cease to apply after death, the protections provided by the right of publicity and copyright have continued vitality even after the person ceases to be. In recent years, moreover, these rights have grown in strength and duration, providing posthumous protections never before seen in history.

The expansion of the legal doctrines of copyright and right of publicity have often been couched in terms of protecting the dead. The protections offered by these doctrines, however, are strictly limited to economic, as opposed to reputational, interests. Although there is some overlap between the two, they are far from coextensive. Indeed, there are many situations where the furtherance of a person's economic interest can harm his or her reputation. This is less likely to happen in countries that provide, in addition to rights of publicity, more direct protections for the reputations of artists through the concept of moral rights.

The Right of Publicity

The right of publicity is described in the law as the rights of an individual to own, protect, and profit from the commercial value of his or her name, picture, and likeness and to prevent others from unfairly appropriating this value for their commercial benefit.[37]

The right of publicity was born as a component of the right of privacy, laid out by Brandies and Warren in their seminal article. As the law developed, however, the right of publicity became its own standalone right that became much more powerful in both scope and duration than any of the other branches of privacy protection.

As originally conceived, the right of publicity protected individuals' privacy by protecting them from having their identities used in advertisements without their permission. One of the first cases brought under this claim was in 1902 by Abigail Roberson, a young woman whose picture was used by a flour company on posters (with the double-entendre slogan "Flour of the Family" under her picture) and distributed to twenty-five thousand stores, warehouses, and saloons. Roberson claimed that as a result of this unauthorized use of her picture in the advertisement, she was "greatly humiliated by the scoffs and jeers" of people who recognized her face.[38] Although her suit was unsuccessful (the court refused to recognize the interest in the absence of legislation), the public outcry from this decision caused the New York legislature to enact a statute in 1905 explicitly prohibiting the use of a name, portrait, or picture of any person for advertising purposes without the person's consent.

In other states, courts developed a right of publicity in the absence of legislation. Thus, shortly after the *Roberson* decision in New York, a similar case arose in Georgia when an insurance company used a picture of a little-known artist, Paolo Pavesich, in an advertisement for the company's insurance. In addition to the picture, the advertisement included this supposed testimonial: "In my healthy and productive period of life I bought insurance in the New England Mutual Life Insurance Co., of Boston, Mass., and to-day my family is protected and I am drawing an annual dividend on my paid-up policies." Pavesich had never purchased life insurance from the company, nor had he agreed to the use of his picture. He filed suit complaining that the advertisement caused him great embarrassment among his friends. The court, in finding for Pavesich, recognized his interest as stemming from the right to control his privacy: "The right to withdraw from the public gaze at such times as a person may see fit, when his presence in public is not demanded by any rule of law, is also embraced within the right of personal liberty." The *Pavesich* case was the first judicial case to explicitly respect this right of publicity.[39]

Although these early cases and the legislation they spawned were sufficient to address the concerns of private individuals seeking to stay out of the public eye, they were ill-suited to address the needs of another group of individuals—namely, those who wanted to control (and profit from) the marketing of their image rather than merely prevent it. The 1953 case of *Haelan Laboratories v. Topps Chewing Gum, Inc.* illustrates this limitation.[40] The case arose from the fact that baseball players had granted one chewing gum company the exclusive right to use the players' pictures on baseball cards. Another chewing gum company subsequently produced its own baseball cards with pictures of the same baseball players. Although New York had a statutory right of privacy at that time, it did not cover this situation. The right of privacy could not be asserted by the company that had purchased the images since the right of privacy was seen as personal to the baseball players and therefore not capable of assignment. Moreover, since the players' reputational interest had already been waived when they consented to appear on the cards of the first company, their privacy could not have been harmed by the subsequent exposure, and therefore they could presumably not sue on their own behalf either.

To address this difficulty and to bring the right of publicity more in line with the market, the New York court moved away from viewing the right of publicity as a purely personal interest protecting a person's reputation and reframed the interest as being more akin to property, which was thus capable of assignment: "We think that in addition to and independent of that right of privacy . . . a man has a right in the publicity value of his photograph. . . . Whether it be labelled a 'property' right is immaterial; for here, as often elsewhere, the tag 'property' simply symbolizes the fact that courts enforce a claim which has pecuniary worth."[41]

This shift in conceptualization—from a personal interest to a property interest—may have seemed insignificant at the time, but it transformed the legal landscape and paved the way for a new billion-dollar industry.

The Effect of Identity as Property

This new conception of the right of publicity as a property interest brought about several functional changes. First, it is much easier to assert rights with respect to property interests as opposed to personal rights. In order to enforce a claim based on invasion of privacy, a person has to prove that he or she has suffered damages as a result of the invasion. When it comes to property, however, the law essentially presumes damages whenever a person's property is used without permission.

Moreover, once the right of publicity was designated as an economic property interest—instead of a mere right to withdraw from the public gaze—it became capable of being owned as a corporate asset. Today ownership of celebrity identities is big business. To get a sense of the extent of this phenomenon, one need look no further than Indiana, corporate headquarters of CMG Worldwide (and not coincidentally, the state with some of the most extensive protections for rights of publicity).[42] CMG owns the rights of publicity of hundreds of individuals, including the actors James Dean, Ingrid Bergman, Bette Davis, and Marlon Brando, musicians such as Duke Ellington, Chuck Berry, Ella Fitzgerald, Billie Holiday, and Don McLean, the sports legends Babe Ruth, Jackie Robinson, Joe Louis, Lou Gehrig, and Jesse Owens, and even historical figures, including Malcolm X, Rosa Parks, Amelia Earhart, Lee Strasberg, Mark Twain, and Frank Lloyd Wright.

Once the right of publicity became a valuable corporate asset, pressure was brought to bear to increase the value of this asset. This resulted in the growth of the right of publicity in both scope and duration.

The first way in which the right of publicity grew was in its scope. As originally established, the right of publicity protected against unauthorized appropriation of a person's name or image. As an economic interest, however, it has expanded to protect far more tangential characteristics. As one scholar has described this transition:

Originally developed primarily to deal with an unauthorized use of a person's name or picture in advertising that suggested the individual's endorsement of a product, the right of publicity has been greatly expanded in the twentieth century. It is no longer limited to the name or likeness of an individual, but now extends to a person's nickname, signature, physical pose, characterizations, singing style, vocal characteristics, body parts, frequently used phrases, car, performance style, mannerisms, and gestures, provided that these are distinctive and publicly identified with the person claiming the right.[43]

Today virtually anything suggestive of a famous person is likely protected by the right of publicity. For example, the late-night talk show host Johnny Carson successfully sued to stop a portable toilet company from using the phrase "Here's Johnny," and the television game show model Vanna White successfully sued to stop a commercial in which a robot in an evening dress and blonde wig turned letters on a mock game show. In addition, the singer Bette Midler was able to stop a car company from using a singer in an advertisement who sang in a similar style to Midler, and Jacqueline Kennedy Onassis was able to enjoin an advertisement that used a model who looked like Onassis.[44]

The other dimension in which the right of publicity has grown is in terms of duration. When the right of publicity was a personal reputational right of the individual, it ended at the person's death (like the right of privacy and the tort of defamation). However, as an economic interest—capable of being bought and sold—there was soon pressure for the right of publicity to acquire other attributes of property—notably, the right to be transmitted at death.[45] Today the right to transmit the right of publicity at death is recognized explicitly by statute or common law in nineteen states.[46] Only two states, New York and Wisconsin, appear to specifically preclude, as a matter of statutory or common law, a postmortem right of publicity.[47]

Where states have recognized a right of publicity that survives death, they have taken approaches to the issue of duration ranging from ten years to a century. The most common provision provides for the right to last fifty years after the person's death. Tennessee (former home of Elvis

Presley) provides a potentially endless right of publicity because it allows the right to continue indefinitely for so long as there is commercial exploitation of the right.[48]

The differing treatment of traditional reputational interests and the right of publicity has produced some anomalous results. Because rights of privacy and claims for defamation terminate at a person's death, the law provides no restrictions on the publication of the most intimate facts about a person's life or protections against publication of lies—regardless of how intentional or malicious. Yet putting a person's image on a T-shirt or greeting card can be prohibited for decades after his or her death. Thus, newspapers, magazines, and books can publish bald-faced lies about Elvis and disclose the most intimate facts about his life, and no one has standing to object. But Elvis impersonators cannot perform without prior approval from CKX, Inc., the multimillion-dollar corporation that owns Elvis's right of publicity.[49]

Problems with a Descendible Right of Publicity

The establishment of the right of publicity as a property right, combined with the growth of the breadth and duration of this right, provides benefits to the heirs of celebrities who want to obtain maximum market value from the celebrity identity as well as the corporate entities that have acquired many of these rights. At the same time, this expansion of the right of publicity imposes significant costs on society and has the potential to harm the very celebrities the law was purportedly designed to protect. The social costs of the right of publicity are imposed both on future would-be celebrities as well as on the public at large.

First, the granting of exclusive proprietary interests in celebrity identities fails to take into account the way that these identities themselves are built on other celebrity identities from the past. As one scholar has noted, almost all celebrities owe at least part of their persona to people and cultural images that have gone before them, elements of which they rely on to build public recognition and appreciation.[50] Another scholar has described stars and their fame as a form of cultural bricolage that improvises with a social history of symbolic forms: "How much does Elvis Costello owe to Buddy Holly, Prince to Jimi Hendrix, or Michael Jackson to Diana Ross? Take the image of Madonna, an icon whose meaning and value lie partially in its evocation and ironic reconfiguration of several twentieth-century sex-goddesses and ice-queens (Marilyn Monroe obviously, but also Jean Harlow, Greta Garbo, and Marlene Dietrich) that speaks with multiple tongues to diverse audiences."[51]

Granting celebrities and their heirs the right to exclusively control these identities is to give disproportionate benefit to the most recent incarnations of these images and to deny their use to future generations. "If we grant Madonna exclusive property rights in her image, we simultaneously make it difficult for others to appropriate those same resources for new ends, and we freeze the Madonna constellation itself. Future artists, writers, and performers will be unable to draw creatively upon the cultural and historical significance of the Madonna montage without seeking the consent of the celebrity, her estate, or its assigns, who may well deny such consent or demand exorbitant royalties."[52] The effect of this is that the public loses "the rich heritage of its culture, the rich presence of new works derived from that culture, and the rich promise of works to come."[53]

Given the breadth of the right of publicity—including practically any attribute that calls to mind the particular individual—the effect of the growth of the right of publicity is deeply threatening to the creative enterprise as a whole. An early critic of these expanding rights described the negative effects on both performers and the society at large:

> From the standpoint of performers . . . the right to perform in the popular genre or style is essential. Freedom of a performer to earn a living by adopting—either consciously or because he is "influenced" or simply "with it"—current modes and styles which may be widely or even uniformly demanded is, indeed, imperative. How else can he support himself and develop? *Any* limitation upon absolute freedom of performance—while it might result in short-lived bonanzas for one or two performers—would self evidently be stultifying to performers as a class.

Even more disturbing than the effect on performers is the broader impact on society:

From the standpoint of the audience, society at large, and cultural growth, encroachment on the freedom of performance would be destructive both qualitatively and quantitatively. Consider any artist, musician, or performer of any era and ponder what his oeuvre would have amounted to had he been precluded from utilizing the brush techniques, color principles, scales, meters, cadences, sounds, moods and methods—in short, the styles —of those who had gone before. Would the classical periods of music and painting have been limited to but one producer each? Would Presley have been foreclosed as an imitator or would he have had the right to foreclose those who came after him? Would the lost generation of American writers have wasted itself in litigation to determine who "got with it" first? Indeed, could there have been a Renaissance? Would we have had a Brahms, a Rubens, a Steinbeck? Or, for that matter, a Sinatra or Fifth Dimension?[54]

Another problem with granting these broad rights of publicity is that they limit the public's ability to create alternate meanings than those put forth in the dominant culture. Michael Madow describes a situation involving John Wayne that well illustrates this tension. After John Wayne's death, his family testified in favor of a statute that would have allowed them to inherit Wayne's right of publicity. In support of their argument they told of a use of John Wayne's image on a greeting card sold in gay bookstores that they found highly offensive:

> The card bears a picture of John Wayne, wearing cowboy hat and bright red lipstick, above the caption, "It's such a bitch being butch." Wayne's children, among others, objected to the card not only on the ground that its sellers were making money from The Duke's image—money that should go to them, or, in this case, to the charity of their choosing. They objected also, indeed primarily, because in their view the card was "tasteless" and demeaned their father's (hard-earned) conservative macho image. . . .
>
> The particular greeting card that Wayne's children and others objected to so strenuously represents an even more subversive inflection of Wayne's image. The card uses his image to inter-

rogate and challenge mainstream conceptions of masculinity and heterosexuality. It recodes Wayne's image so as to make it carry a cultural meaning that presumably works for gay men, among others, but which Wayne's children (and no doubt many of his fans) find deeply offensive. If the New York Legislature were to make John Wayne's right of publicity descendible, however, it would confer on Wayne Enterprises the power to determine that this particular appropriation of the John Wayne image is "illegitimate," and to enforce that determination by denying a license to the greeting card maker. Wayne Enterprises would henceforth have the power to fix, or at least try to fix, the meaning that "John Wayne" has in our culture: his meaning for us.[55]

These problems are all exacerbated by the lengthening of the period of survival of the right of publicity. It is one thing to impose these costs on society for the life of the decedent, or even ten years after death, and quite another to have them imposed for a hundred years or in perpetuity.

Surprisingly, in addition to imposing costs on society, the descendible right of publicity can impose costs on the celebrities themselves. This cost is likely to be particularly high on those celebrities who would prefer to not exploit their right of publicity.

Although the right of publicity is often described as the ability to *control* the use of a person's identity after death, because this right focuses on the economic value of a person's identity, it provides only a particular type of control. Namely, it provides control for heirs who want to exploit the maximum commercial value of a person's identity. It provides little control for decedents or heirs who want to *refrain* from marketing the individual's right of publicity. The reason for this is twofold. First, as we saw in chapter 3, the law generally looks with disfavor on the destruction of property—even intangible property, such as a right of publicity. So if an individual left instructions that his or her name or image could not be marketed after death, it is unlikely that an American court would enforce this request.

Second, because of the interplay of the estate tax system and the right of publicity, heirs may be financially obligated to exploit the decedent's right of publicity in order to pay the estate taxes associated with the interest.[56] The estate tax is imposed on all property that is transmittable at death, measured at its highest market value. Therefore, when state laws create a descendible right of publicity, they create an asset that is subject to tax in the dead person's estate at its highest market value, regardless of whether the estate chooses to exploit the right of publicity. The effect of this rule is that estates of celebrities are subject to tax based on the maximum exploitation value of their right of publicity. If that value were determined to be ten million dollars (a conservative estimate: Albert Einstein's name produced eighteen million dollars of income in 2007 from Baby Einstein products alone), then at a 45 percent estate tax rate, the heirs of the estate would need to pay $4.5 million on the value of the name. If the estate has no other assets, then it could be required to market the name in order to recognize the value necessary to pay the associated estate taxes.

Ironically, the greatest burdens associated with this phenomenon are likely to be imposed on those individuals who were most protective of their identities during life. This is because the lack of exploitation during life would increase the market value of their identity (since it hadn't been sullied by overuse), and because it was not exploited during life, it is more likely that there would be insufficient estate assets to pay the taxes on the unexploited right of publicity.

Consider the case of J. D. Salinger, the famously reclusive author of *Catcher in the Rye*. How much would a publisher pay to be able to take the J. D. Salinger name, append it to ghostwritten books, and pass it off on the public as newly found books of J. D. Salinger? If this scenario sounds far-fetched, consider the real-life case of V. C. Andrews. Andrews had written several highly successful books (in a genre known as "children in jeopardy") and had contracts with a publisher to write several more when she suffered an untimely death. The publisher, not wanting to give up on a winner, acquired the right to use Andrews's name from the Andrews estate and hired a ghostwriter to create several more books to be published under the V. C. Andrews name. Numerous books were successfully passed off on the public as V. C. Andrews books (under the terms of the agreement, the ghostwriter was obligated to keep secret the fact that those books were not written by V. C. Andrews).

In the Andrews case, the estate was arguably appropriately subject to tax on her name because it was marketed by her estate. Under basic principles of tax law, however, an estate is subject to tax on the market value even if it doesn't sell the name. In the Salinger case, if a publisher would pay ten million dollars for the right to use Salinger's name on other books, then his estate would need to pay $4.5 million to the federal government even if they refused to participate. The absence of other assets in Salinger's estate would likely close off that choice and force the marketing of the name.

Of course, if there were no descendible right of publicity, then the celebrity identity would become part of the public domain—available to anyone who chooses to use it. That use, however, would not come with the seeming approval of the decedent or his or her heirs.

Copyright

Woody Allen once quipped, "I don't want to achieve immortality through my work. I want to achieve it through not dying." Although others may share the comedian's preference, none to date have achieved it, leaving copyright as the primary vehicle through which American artists and writers can "live on" after death.

Like the right of publicity, copyright has grown in scope and duration. In the earliest days of the Republic, copyright applied only to books, maps, and charts and lasted for just fourteen years.[57] Today copyright applies to all creative expressions and gives control over the original as well as all derivative works until seventy years after the death of the creator. Although this expansion has served to increase the economic value of copyrights, it has not been without costs. The extension of copyright has limited public access to these creations and curtailed the creation of other works.

What Is Copyright?

Copyright is the protection in American law that is provided for creative works. Copyright law gives copyright holders the exclusive right to control creative work for a set time, after which the work falls into the public domain and becomes available for all to use in whatever way they like. Copyright protection was designed to serve two purposes: to give a limited monopoly in order to provide an economic incentive for authors to publish books and disseminate ideas to the public, and to ensure that the works enter the public domain after the author's exclusive, but limited, rights have expired.[58]

Many people think of copyright as something that is held by individual writers and artists, but it is far more likely that these interests will be held by corporations such as Disney and Warner Brothers. Copyright law supports this by providing that works created under an employment agreement are considered to be owned by the employer and not the creator. Moreover, copyright interests are freely transferable, and many interests that we associate with an individual are in fact owned by large corporate entities.

As stated, copyright protection originally applied only to books, maps, and charts. Today copyright law protects the expression of ideas in whatever form they are expressed. Stories, essays, poetry, paintings, photography, film, musical compositions and dance, even style of performance, are all protected by copyright.[59] Moreover, because copyright automatically attaches to any work on creation—there are no longer any formal requirements, such as registration—copyright protection extends to more casual creations as well, such as letters, e-mails, diaries, and even shopping lists.[60]

The scope of copyright protection has expanded in other ways as well. As originally conceived, copyright protected only against exact duplication of a work and gave the copyright holder only the right to control exact duplication—giving rise to the term "*copy*-right."[61] Because of this limited scope, even abridgments or translations of a work to another language were not protected by the original copyright statute. Over the twentieth century, copyright law was extended to afford the copyright holder control over all works derived from the original, as well as the original itself. This expansion of copyright provided protections for far more than abridgments and translations. It allowed copyright holders to cast a broad protective swathe over their original creations and gave them the economic power to leverage their creations into large economic empires. Through modern copyright law, George Lucas, the filmmaker and creator of *Star Wars,* has been able to create an economic empire first by controlling the right to make all subsequent *Star Wars* movies and then by using his copyright protection to earn profits from *Star Wars* toys, clothing, books, and games.

Copyright and Immortality

Copyright in American law was always designed to be for a limited duration. This is provided for in the Constitution, which specifically provides that "Congress shall have power . . . [t]o promote the progress of science and useful arts by securing *for limited times* to authors and inventors the exclusive right to their respective writings and discoveries."[62] However, over the course of this country's history, "limited times" has come to cover longer and longer periods.

The first copyright law was specifically designed to last no longer than the life of the author. Thomas Jefferson proposed a copyright term of nineteen years after consulting actuarial tables to calculate how long a person was likely to live.[63] The original copyright term accomplished this goal by having a relatively short initial term (fourteen years with the possibility of renewal for an additional fourteen-year term) and more directly by allowing extension of the term only if the creator was still living.

Although the copyright term was subsequently extended by legislation several times—from twenty-eight years in 1790 to forty-two years in 1831 to fifty-six years in 1909—not until 1976 did copyright law explicitly provide for a term that survived the creator's death. The 1976 Copyright Act established a copyright term of the life of the author plus fifty years. The reason for this was to explicitly allow copyright interests to benefit not just the original creator but also his or her children for their lifetimes.

In 1998, the duration of copyright was extended again by the Sonny Bono Copyright Term Extension Act, which added another twenty years —making the duration of a copyright the life of the author plus seventy years after death. Some legal scholars believe that this most recent extension exceeded Congress's power under the Constitution. Nonetheless, in *Eldred v. Ashcroft* the Supreme Court ruled that this extension did not violate the limited period requirement any more than did the earlier extensions to copyright law enacted in 1831, 1909, and 1976.[64]

Why do we limit copyright at all? After all, if it is a product of a person's labor, why doesn't the law treat artistic creations the same as tangible ones? We don't limit the duration of ownership of a handcrafted jewelry box, so why do we limit the duration of ownership of a poem?

Many artists have argued that copyright should be perpetual. The author Samuel Clemens, better known by his pen name Mark Twain, testified before Congress in 1906 that a time limitation on copyright was both unfair and unnecessary because in the vast majority of cases the public will lose interest long before the copyright term expires: "I made an estimate once . . . as to the output of books, and by my estimate we had issued and published in this country since the Declaration of Independence 220,000 books. What was the use of protecting those books by copyright? They are all gone. They had all perished before they were 10 years old. There is only about one book in a thousand that can outlive the forty two years of copyright. Therefore, why put a limit at all? You might just as well limit a family to 22. It will take care of itself."[65]

Although the notion of perpetual copyright has some initial appeal, it fails to take into account the breadth of copyright protection and the attendant cost on society that copyright protection can impose. Unlike tangible property, copyright protection does more than secure the rights to the original work; it also extends to all creative works that are derived from the original. This ability to keep others from using and building on protected works can impose significant costs on society at large as well as on other artists.

Consider the case of the Irish writer James Joyce, considered by many one of the greatest writers in the English language. Joyce is so venerated that Ireland established a national holiday on 16 June called Bloomsday in honor of Joyce's most esteemed book *Ulysses,* which follows the character Leopold Bloom over a single day, 16 June 1904. The day is celebrated in Ireland and around the world with live readings of Joyce's work as well as other festivities. In addition, Joyce's work is the subject of extraordinary scholarly interest.

Nonetheless, in recent years, a cloud has hung over performances of Joyce's work and scholarly research on Joyce's life. The reason is that Stephen Joyce, the writer's grandson, still holds the copyright on Joyce's published and unpublished work (and because of the extension of the copyright law, he will continue to do so for decades), and he has exercised his control with a vengeance. D. T. Max explored the extent of the younger Joyce's stranglehold on the James Joyce legacy in a 2006 article in the *New Yorker:*

> In 2004, the centenary of Bloomsday, Stephen threatened the Irish government with a lawsuit if it staged any Bloomsday readings; the readings were cancelled. He warned the National Library of Ireland that a planned display of his grandfather's manuscripts violated his copyright. (The Irish Senate passed an emergency amendment to thwart him.) His antagonism led the Abbey Theatre to cancel a production of Joyce's play "Exiles," and he told Adam Harvey, a performance artist who had simply memorized a portion of "Finnegans Wake" in expectation of reciting it onstage, that he had likely "already infringed" on the estate's copyright. . . . Stephen has also attempted to impede the publication of dozens of scholarly works on James Joyce. He rejects nearly every request to quote from unpublished letters. Last year, he told a prominent Joyce scholar that he was no longer granting permissions to quote from any of Joyce's writings.[66]

Another scholar has described the Joyce situation as follows:

> The James Joyce Estate, whose sole beneficiary is the author's grandson[,] has chosen to take such an approach, either refusing permissions, or demanding above market royalties for adaptations and publications, even those that were in the works before the retroactive term extensions gave the Estate a new lease on life. Since 1995 the Joyce Estate has forbidden the publication of new print and digital editions of Joyce's work, prevented or exorbitantly charged for public readings, translations and inclusions of excerpts within anthologies, and enjoined the performance of numerous musical adaptations. In 1998 the Estate even sued the sponsors of a nonprofit round the world reading of Ulysses that had been webcast on Bloomsday of that year.[67]

Sometimes Stephen Joyce frames his refusals in terms of protecting the spirit of his grandfather, and at other times he is more explicitly capricious. As the younger Joyce wrote in denying permission to allow an Irish composer to use eighteen words from *Finnegans Wake* in a three-and-a-half-minute choral composition, Joyce explained, "To put it politely, mildly, my wife and I don't like your music."[68] Of course, none of this would have been possible in the day when copyright protection lasted fourteen years after creation.

In addition to limiting access to original works, the extension of copyright inhibits the creation of new works that build on existing works. The tradition of creating new works based on existing works is lengthy and rich. Mark Twain himself used this technique in writing one of his own classics, *A Connecticut Yankee in King Arthur's Court*, which overtly drew on the King Arthur legends. (Luckily for him, the King Arthur stories were not eligible for the type of perpetual copyright that Clemens advocated for in regard to his own work.) Other authors who benefited from the lack of copyright protection include Shakespeare and Milton, both of whom drew explicitly on existing stories.[69] The musical *West Side Story*, a celebrated artistic creation in its own right, was based on Shakespeare's *Romeo and Juliet*. The Disney Corporation has arguably been the most financially successful example of an entity benefitting from historically limited copyright protection—allowing Disney to draw freely from such stories as Snow White, Cinderella, and Pinocchio—because Jacob and Wilhelm Grimm did not have copyright protection. As the professor and lawyer Lawrence Lessig points out, the effect of copyright extension is that "no one can do to Disney as Disney did to the Brothers Grimm."[70]

Now that copyright protections have been extended, the ability of people to build on prior works has been further limited. Consider the several artists who have attempted to build on the Pulitzer Prize–winning 1936 novel *Gone with the Wind*. Its author, Margaret Mitchell, never wrote a sequel to her book and died in 1949. Because the work remains under copyright, Mitchell's heirs can prevent the creation of other works that build on the original story or characters—even if the new author clearly designates his or her work as unauthorized. Mitchell's heirs have aggressively asserted this right. They successfully stopped the distribution of a book called *The Winds of Tara* that picked up the story where the original left off. They also attempted to stop publication of another book called *The Wind Done Gone* that retold the story of *Gone with the Wind* from the point of view of the mulatto slave half-sister of Scarlett O'Hara. Although that book was eventually published, it was only after years of expensive litigation. A less tenacious (and less financially well-off) publisher would likely not have pursued the issue. The Mitchell heirs also successfully stopped the production of a musical parody called *Scarlett Fever*.[71] We will never know whether *Scarlett Fever* would have been the next *West Side Story*.

For proponents of copyright, issues involving access to the works of James Joyce and the ability to write a sequel or a play based on a copyrighted work may seem a small price to pay for a system that increases the value of private interests. However, the expansion of copyright is subject to a more fundamental problem: it fails to consider the way that all artistic creations are built on other artistic creations.

As Mark Rose explains in *Authors and Owners: The Invention of Copyright:* "Copyright is founded on the concept of the unique individual who creates something original and is entitled to reap a profit from those labors. But these assumptions obscure important truths about the processes of cultural production."[72] In fact, all creative expressions are built upon other creative expressions. In the words of literary theorist Northrop Frye, "Poetry can only be made out of other poems; novels out of other novels."[73]

Copyright law purports to solve this problem by carving out space for other people's creative endeavors in two ways. The first is that copyright does not protect ideas; it protects only the particular expression of the idea (this is called the idea-expression dichotomy). This allows other artists to build on the same ideas, as long as they express them differently. The second protection is that people are allowed to make "fair use" of otherwise copyrighted material.[74] Fair use is designed to protect such things as research, education, criticism, parodies, and other limited uses.

Although these doctrines theoretically protect subsequent creators from the reaches of copyright, this protection is not as robust as it might appear. The reason is that these exceptions are difficult to apply and copyright law imposes a heavy cost on those who miscalculate its application. The idea-expression dichotomy is difficult to apply because the distinction between an idea and an expression of an idea is not inherently obvious.[75] Fair use is difficult to determine because the doctrine's application is dependent on a highly contextual, equitable multifactor test whose results are notoriously difficult to predict.[76] As one scholar has noted, in every fair use case decided by the Supreme Court, the trial court ruled one way, the appellate court reversed, and the Supreme Court reversed yet again.[77] The cost of miscalculation, moreover, is high. If a person uses copyrighted material in the belief that it is covered by fair use, he or she is still subject to injunction, statutory damages, and significant legal fees. Given the difficulties of applying the copyright exceptions combined with the significant cost of miscalculation, it is no wonder that copyright law has been found to impose a chilling effect on creative expression.[78] Many works that would fall well within the recognized exceptions to copyright are not pursued for fear of lawsuit.

Legal scholars have made a number of proposals to improve the fair use exception: some have suggested that the fair use exception should increase over time such that the older the work is, the greater the scope of fair use should be, while other scholars have suggested ways to make the fair use exception more certain and therefore more usable by consumers.[79] Although these approaches differ, any of them would be a significant improvement over the status quo.

Copyright and Reputation

American copyright law is designed primarily to allow writers and artists to recognize the economic value of their creations. Through copyright, the expression of ideas is converted into property, like shares of stock, capable of being sold during life or transmitted at death. Thus musicians Elvis Presley and Kurt Cobain and the creator of *Peanuts*, Charles Schulz, are all able to continue to generate significant revenue after their death by virtue of the copyright in their creations.

For many artists, however, their relation to their creations is very different from the relation of a person to a share of stock. For these artists, their creations are extensions of their identity, and their desire to control their creations stems from a desire to control their reputation as an artist.

To what extent does American copyright law allow artists to control their reputational interests in connection with their creations? The answer for most artists is very little. The reason is that copyright law is designed to protect copyright holders, as opposed to the original artists who create the copyrighted work. Copyright interests are freely transferable, and once copyright has been transferred, the artist retains no residual right in the work.

The case of *Geisel v. Poynter Products* illustrates some of the difficulties for artists that can arise after they have transferred their copyright. This case involved the work of Theodor Geisel (better known as Dr. Seuss). Early in his career, Geisel was a freelance artist who sold some cartoons to a magazine in 1932. Years later, when Dr. Seuss had become a world-famous artist and author, the magazine publisher took the cartoons and commissioned the creation of dolls based on the images, marketing them with the name "Dr. Seuss." Geisel filed a lawsuit complaining that the dolls were "tasteless, unattractive and of poor quality" and that the sale of them held him up to ridicule and contempt in his profession as a distinguished artist and author.[80] Nonetheless, the court ruled that when Geisel transferred the signed cartoons to the publisher, he also transferred the copyright in both his name and signature, including all rights to develop the copyright in whatever way the purchaser wanted.

Moral Rights: A Different Approach to Artists' Rights

Under American law, artists' interest in their work is protected by the copyright regime. Although these rights have extended in scope and duration, the focus of copyright protection is on economic rather than reputational value.

In contrast to the American system, many countries provide artists with two legal regimes to protect their work: copyright and moral rights (also called "droit morale"). Moral rights exist throughout Europe as well as other parts of the world, including Japan, Mexico, Canada, and Nigeria.[81] France is the foremost defender of moral rights. The rights take different forms in different countries but in all cases are concerned primarily with preserving an artist's reputation and vision for his or her work.

Moral rights protect the personality of the artist and the integrity of his or her work. The term "moral rights" refers to a collection of rights, including most prominently the right of paternity, which is the right to have one's name associated with a work (or not associated with a work) and the right to control the integrity of the work. The right of paternity has allowed ghostwriters to insist that their name be associated with a work, even though they contractually agreed that their name would not appear. The right of integrity has allowed the rights of the original artist, and his or her heirs, to continue even after the copyright has been sold. Had the *Geisel* case occurred in a jurisdiction that recognized moral rights, Dr. Seuss would have retained the rights to control (and prevent) both the transformation of his work from two-dimensional cartoon to a doll, as well as the association of his name with the dolls—even though he had transferred the copyright.

Moral rights cast an even broader net than copyright. In most countries, moral rights are perpetual. They allow heirs to exert control over artistic creations long after the artist's death.[82]

A Tale of Two Countries

The contrast between the protections provided by moral rights as opposed to copyright was made vividly apparent in the case of film colorization. In the 1980s, Turner Entertainment Company began colorizing its inventory of movies in order to make them more popular with contemporary viewers. Traditionalists (and many directors) complained that colorization destroyed the artistic integrity of the films and even tried to get Congress to enact legislation to address the problem. Yet their complaints were groundless in the United States, where copyright holders are given near absolute control over their copyrighted property.

One artist who was particularly upset about colorization was the director John Huston. He testified in Congress against colorization and was reputed to have said, "It's not color, it's like pouring 40 tablespoons of sugar water over a roast." Despite his anger, Huston was powerless to do anything to stop colorization of his films from occurring since TEC owned the copyright on his movies. Had the case remained in the United States that would have been the end of the story. Because TEC owned the copyright to its films, it could do with them what it wanted.

However, TEC wanted to distribute its colorized films in other parts of the world. To do so, it had to contend with an additional legal regime: moral rights. To test its power to distribute the films, TEC went to France—the country with the strongest moral rights. (Under TEC's theory, if the company could make it there, it would make it anywhere). To test its case, TEC arranged for a local French television station to broadcast a colorized version of John Huston's film *The Asphalt Jungle.*

Although Huston was no longer living, his children brought suit against the television station, asking the French court to stop the television station from showing the film. Here the result was quite different from the United States. The French court ruled that regardless of TEC's copyright interest in the film, John Huston, as the film's director, retained moral rights in his creation. These rights could not have been transferred to TEC because Huston did not have the power to transmit his moral rights except to his heirs at death. Moreover, these moral rights never expire, so his heirs could continue to exert his interest in order to protect Huston's reputation after death.

Moral Rights Come to the United States

Congress adopted a form of moral rights legislation for the first time in 1998. One reason that it did so was to conform to its obligation under the Berne Convention, an international treaty that requires all signatory states to enact statutes protecting artists' moral rights. Unlike moral rights statutes in France and other European countries, however, the moral rights statute Congress enacted was carefully drafted so as not to step on the toes of the multitude of corporate copyright holder interests. Thus, the moral rights statute in the United States applies only to paintings and other visual arts of fewer than two hundred copies and protects only against intentional distortions that harm the reputation of the artist and the destruction of works of recognized stature. Most important, the rights provided for under the Visual Artists Rights Act (VARA) do not survive the artist's life.

CONCLUSION

Life is fleeting and we know it. This is the fundamental truth of human existence, and managing this reality shapes everything we do.

We see this most tangibly in the common practice of placing a stone marker at the location of a person's physical remains. Yet there are numerous intangible examples of this as well, including religious and secular days of remembrance that send the message: "You will live on after your death."

Sociologists have noted that the activities people value most are those with the capacity to transcend death: having children (who themselves have the capacity to have children), creating art, building skyscrapers, adding a link in the chain of knowledge, and fighting for causes they believe in.

The law plays a critical role in enabling people to live on following death. Whenever the law provides a mechanism for enforcing people's wishes—whether it is with respect to their body, property, or reputation—it gives people a degree of immortality.

Yet there is an inevitable trade-off. Whenever we grant rights to the dead, we invariably affect the living. How the law treats bodies after death (as well as the legal definition of death itself) has a direct impact on the availability of organs for transplant. The amount of control that a person is given over his or her property after death affects the ability of the living to use or access that property. Legal protections for the reputation of the dead limit the ability of the living to write history and biographies.

Different Societies, Different Choices

While the desire for immortality is universal, societies have responded differently in terms of how they balance the interests of the living and the dead. The particular trade-offs that the law makes reflect what
the society most values. We see this in differing privacy rights of the dead:
the dignity of the dead is paramount in European law, whereas American
law favors the free expression rights of the living. In practice, this difference was evident in the coverage of the execution of Saddam Hussein. In
the United States, the execution was widely broadcasted on television in
all of its gruesome details, whereas in some European countries, networks
were directed to be mindful of how they showed the events in order to
preserve Hussein's personal dignity.

In addition to reflecting *what* the society most values, the law also reflects *who* the society most values. The Polish sociologist Zygmunt Bauman explains in his book *Mortality, Immortality and Other Life Strategies*
that although a common feature of all societies is that they provide some
level of immortality for all of their members, we can learn what any one
society most values by examining to whom it grants particularized immortality. Outside the context of law, examples of particularized immortality are all around us, including halls of fame for sports and entertainment figures, the naming of city streets (and sometimes even whole cities)
after esteemed citizens, lengthy newspaper obituaries for the renowned,
and, for the most revered, setting aside an annual day in their honor.[1]

Applying Bauman's insight to law, we see that here, too, societies provide particularized immortality in the form of posthumous rights to those
most valued within that society. Consider the allocation of posthumous
rights between artists and purchasers of the art: Who ultimately controls
the fate of artistic creations? French culture has a long tradition of valu-
ing artists; therefore, it is not surprising that in France, artists have a wide
range of posthumous rights that allow them to control their creations
and reputations after death. In the United States, although we may not
explicitly say who we most value, the law speaks volumes when it grants
greater rights to an owner of art than it does to its creator. Another example lies in the legal treatment of dead bodies, which has a history
replete with double standards: the bodies of the indigent were freely

handed over first for medical research and then for organ transplants, whereas the law safeguarded bodies of the wealthy from the same fates.

The Rising Power of the American Dead

American law grants more rights to the dead than any other country in the world. Moreover, it grants much greater rights today than it has in the past. Thus, whereas previously people could generally control property in private trusts for no longer than ninety years after their death, today property can be controlled in perpetuity. Previously people could make outright gifts only to existing charitable organizations; today people can create their own perpetual charitable entities for whatever purpose they choose. Copyright protection was originally structured to last no longer than the life of the author; today it can last up to seventy years after the author's death. Whereas previously the right of publicity ended at death, in many states today it can last fifty or a hundred years, and in at least one state in perpetuity.

This expansion of rights to the dead has a price. Our deference to the wishes of the dead imposes significant costs on living individuals and threatens our most fundamental societal values:

- By expanding the right of publicity in both scope and duration, we freeze out future celebrities' ability to freely develop new personas based on existing archetypes.
- By expanding copyright law without fortifying the fair use exception, we inhibit the public's access to existing works and deprive our culture of new works that artists might create based on those existing works.
- By encouraging charitable giving in the form of perpetual charitable foundations (as opposed to outright bequests), we waste assets in furtherance of perpetuity and starve the known problems of today in order to preserve resources to address the unknown problems of tomorrow.
- By failing to tax inherited wealth and allowing the creation of perpetual private trusts, we allow the dead to impose their wishes on future generations. More troubling, we are allowing them to establish a new aristocracy made up of individuals who will have access to large amounts

of untaxed wealth to meet their every need and desire while being immune from claims of creditors.

Why Have We Allowed This to Occur?

The rising power of the American dead threatens our most fundamental values. This raises the question: Why have we allowed this to occur?

In part, the reason has to do with the stealth nature of these changes. The larger picture has gone unnoticed because change has occurred within discreet areas of the law, and often at the state level. However, there are larger cultural reasons as well.

As a starting point, cultural historians have noted that we as a people are peculiarly anti-death. As the British historian Arnold Toynbee wrote in 1968: "For Americans, death is un-American and an affront to every citizen's inalienable right to life, liberty and the pursuit of happiness."[2] Given Americans' anti-death stance, it is not surprising that American law has embraced legal rules that seem to deny death its ultimate power.

In addition, the United States is a relatively new nation and is distinctly ahistorical. Most other parts of the world have longer histories and people live among constant reminders of their past. In these societies, the risks of allowing values from the past to control the present are more salient. Moreover, other societies have lived through and suffered the burdens of dead hand control. Indeed, in establishing our republic, the founders were mindful of this history and consciously attempted to establish a nation that would be largely free from the strictures of the past. Over time, however, we have forgotten what our founders knew, and today we are re-creating the very world from which they sought to distance themselves.

Finally, the story of the American law of the dead would not be complete without recognition of the effect of money on legislation. It is significant that the areas in which American law has grown most dramatically—dynasty trusts, charitable trusts, copyright, and rights of publicity—not only appeal to individuals' desire to exert posthumous control but also appreciably benefit corporate interests. By using interests of the dead as a decoy, these entities have succeeded in enriching their own property interests. Although financial gain may be the driving force behind these changes, corporations are not the ultimate villains. Businesses are *a*moral, simply doing what our society tells them to do: maximize profit. The blame lies with legislators, who have responded to corporate demands even when they have not best served the needs of American society at large.

When we increase the rights of the dead, we decrease the rights and opportunities for the living. Now is the time to restore the balance to reflect our most fundamental values. Our legacy depends on it.

Introduction

1. Religions have their own conceptions of afterlife and often draw connections between actions of the living and the afterlife of the dead. For example, Orthodox Judaism provides for the eventual physical resurrection of the dead. It is therefore not surprising that Jewish law imposes certain burial obligations on the living (such as avoiding cremation and placing the body in special consecrated ground) that are designed to facilitate eventual resurrection.

2. Thomas Jefferson to Thomas Earle, 1823, in *The Jefferson Cyclopedia*, ed. John P. Foley (New York: Funk and Wagnalls, 1900), entry 3401.

3. This may be changing. In recent years several authors have addressed different aspects of the legal rights of the dead, including Ronald Chester, *From Here to Eternity? Property and the Dead Hand* (Lake Mary, FL: Vandaplas, 2007); Daniel Sperling, *Posthumous Interests: Legal and Ethical Perspectives* (Cambridge: Cambridge University Press, 2008); and Lawrence Friedman, *Dead Hands: A Social History of Wills, Trusts, and Inheritance Law* (Stanford, CA: Stanford University Press, 2009).

4. Jonathan Turley, "King for Sale," *Los Angeles Times,* 22 April 2009, 29; Associated Press, "King Family Gets Fees for Memorial," *Orlando Sentinel,* 18 April 2009, A16.

Chapter 1: Controlling the Body

1. U.S. Constitution, amend. 13.

2. Esther B. Fein, "Bury Lenin? Russian Die-Hards Aghast," *New York Times,* 28 April 1989, A10; C. J. Chivers, "With Lenin's Ideas Dead, What to Do with His Body?" *New York Times,* 5 October 2005, A3; "Lenin's Body May Find New Home in Minsk," *Pravda,* 11 May 2009.

3. Harvey Rachlin, *Lucy's Bones, Sacred Stones, and Einstein's Brain* (New York: Henry Holt, 1996), 203.

4. Sandra West was apparently not alone in this desire to be buried in her car. In 1998, a woman who lived in Tiverton, Rhode Island, was buried in her 1962 Corvair. The engine, steering wheel, and seats were removed to make room for her casket. Janet Kerlin, "Tiverton Woman Buried in Beloved Car," *Associated Press*, 6 May 1998. In another case, a man was buried in his 1984 Corvette. "Buried in Style: Man Gets Wish . . . Interment in His 'Vette," *Associated Press*, 25 May 1994. Russell E. Haddleton, "What to Do with the Body? The Trouble with Postmortem Disposition," *Probate and Property* 20 (November–December 2006).

5. Andrew Buncombe, "Going, Going, Gonzo: Hunter S. Thompson Blasts Off," *Independent*, 22 August 2005; Katharine Q. Seelye, "Ashes-to-Fireworks Send-Off for an 'Outlaw' Writer," *New York Times*, 22 August 2005, A8; "Hunter Thompson's Ashes to Be Shot from Cannon in a Final Farewell Saturday Night," *CBC News*, 20 August 2005.

6. Tom Miller, "Hiking Club Spreads a Little Bit of Charlie on Every Peak," *New York Times*, 25 January 2007, A18.

7. Einstein was always concerned about the fate of his final remains. People treated Einstein as a living monument. He was once mobbed in Geneva, where a crazed young girl tried to snip off a lock of his hair. Such behavior led Einstein to worry about what the public would do to his body after his death. Carolyn Abraham, "My Dad Has Einstein's Brain," *Guardian*, 8 April 2004. See also Rachlin, *Lucy's Bones*, 325.

8. Haddleton, "What to Do with the Body?" 59.

9. *Holland v. Metalious*, 198 A.2d 654 (N.H 1964).

10. *Louisville & N.R. Co. v. Wilson*, 51 S.E. 24, 25 (Ga. 1905).

11. Although many posit that the root of this rule is in the view that the body is sacred, Lori Andrews suggests another possible interpretation: that under English common law, there was a notion that people's bodies belonged to the Crown. This would be consistent with the feudal law that it was a crime to maim oneself because this rendered one less able to fight for the king. Lori Andrews, "Who Owns Your Body? A Patient's Perspective on *Washington University v. Catalona*," *Journal of Legal Medicine and Ethics* 34 (2006): 400.

12. *Williams v. Williams*, 20 Ch. Div. 659.

13. *Williams*, 20 Ch. Div. 659 at 662–63, 665.

14. *Williams*, 20 Ch. Div. 659 at 665.

15. The Fifth Amendment provides that "no person shall be . . . deprived of . . . property, without due process of law; nor shall private property be taken for public use, without just compensation."

16. This has particular significance in the development of laws involving organ donation.

17. When the model and television personality Anna Nicole Smith died in 2007, there was a lengthy trial over who was authorized to make the decision regarding the

disposition of her body: the executor of her will, her mother, or one of the two potential fathers of her newborn daughter. The probate court judge ultimately ruled
that the infant daughter was the appropriate decision-maker. This case was a more
public version of a controversy that has played out since the nation's inception—
fights among family members and others about controlling the disposition of a person's body after death. Frances H. Foster, "Individualized Justice in Disputes over
Dead Bodies," *Vanderbilt Law Review* 61 (2008): 1351.

18. *Ark. Code Ann.* § 20-17-102 (Arkansas); *Colo. Rev. Stat.* § 12-34-204 (Colorado);
Conn. Gen. Stat. § 45a-318 (Connecticut); *Del. Code Ann.* tit. 12, § 262 (2004) (Dela-
ware); *D.C. Code* § 3-413 (District of Columbia); 755 *Ill. Comp. Stat.* 65/40 (Illinois);
Md. Code Ann., [Health-General] § 5-509 (Maryland); *Minn. Stat.* § 149A.80 (Min-
nesota); *Nev. Rev. Stat.* § 451.655 (Nevada); *N.M. Stat.* § 24-12A-1 (New Mexico); *N.C.
Gen. Stat.* § 130A-420 (North Carolina); *Or. Rev. Stat.* § 97.130 (Oregon); *R.I. Gen.
Laws* § 5-33.2-24 (Rhode Island); *S.D. Codified Laws* § 34-26-1 (South Dakota); *Utah
Code Ann.* § 58-9-601 (Utah); *Wash. Rev. Code* § 68.50.160 (Washington).

19. Arizona, *Ariz. Rev. Stat. Ann.* § 36-831.01.

20. Delaware, 12 *Del. Code Ann.,* tit. 12, § 265.

21. States have broad discretion to determine when a medical investigation into
the death of an individual (including autopsy) should be held. See 18 *Am. Jur. 2d
Coroners* § 7. In most states, a medical examiner may review any death that has occurred under violent or criminal circumstances. Likewise, most states provide that a
coroner may investigate any death that occurs "suddenly" when the decedent appeared to be in good health. See, e.g., Florida (*Fla. Stat.* § 406.50); and Virginia (*Va.
Code Ann.* § 32.1-283). Finally, states commonly provide for an autopsy in the event
that the death is considered to have occurred by accident or under any suspicious or
unusual circumstances. See Florida's *Fla. Stat.* § 406.11; and Alaska's *Alaska Stat.* §
12.65.005.

22. See the discussion below on presumed consent statutes.

23. Alison Dundes Renteln, "The Rights of the Dead: Autopsies and Corpse Mis-
management in Multicultural Societies," *South Atlantic Quarterly* 100 (2001): 1006–
7.

24. *Snyder v. Holy Cross Hosp.,* 352 A.2d 334 (Md. App. 1976) (a case in which the
court allowed an autopsy to determine the cause of death, following the sudden and
unexplained death of the father's eighteen-year-old son, who had been in apparent
good health, over the religious objections of the father).

25. Mark A. Hall, Mary Anne Bobinski, and David Orentlicher, *Bioethics and Public Health Law* (New York: Aspen, 2005), 365. See also *Reilly v. City of New York*
(E.D.N.Y. 1992) (holding autopsy laws to be clearly constitutional).

26. Tanya K. Hernández, "The Property of Death," *University of Pittsburgh Law
Review* 60 (1999): 971.

27. The Anna Nicole Smith case is a contemporary example of one of these disputes. *Wynkoop v. Wynkoop* and *Weld v. Walker* are older cases that present almost
identical facts in which a spouse (the wife in Wynkoop and the husband in Weld)

sought to move the body, which had been buried by the next of kin. These cases are discussed in *American Law Review* 14 (1880): 57. Although the facts of each case are almost identical, the courts come out differently in the two cases.

28. James Brooke Little, *The Law of Burial: Including All the Burial Acts as Modified or Affected by the Local Government (England and Wales) Act, 1894* (London: Shaw and Sons, 1894), 11.

29. Sidney Perley, *Mortuary Law* (Boston: George B. Reed, 1896), 31.

30. George Chase, ed., *Commentaries on the Laws of England, in Four Books by Sir William Blackstone* (New York: Banks and Brothers, 1877), 606.

31. *State v. Bradbury,* 9 A.2d 657 (Me. 1939).

32. "Tells of Cremating Body of Sister, 76," *New York Times,* 12 June 1938, 37.

33. *State v. Bradbury,* 9 A.2d 657, 659.

34. Laura Lunger Knoppers, *Constructing Cromwell: Ceremony, Portrait and Print, 1645–1661* (Cambridge: Cambridge University Press, 2000), 182.

35. Act of 22 Geo. 2 c. 37; Michael Sappol, *A Traffic of Dead Bodies: Anatomy and Embodied Social Identity in Nineteenth-Century America* (Princeton, NJ: Princeton University Press, 2002), 100–101.

36. Aaron D. Tward and Hugh A. Patterson, "From Grave Robbing to Gifting: Cadaver Supply in the United States," *Journal of the American Medical Association* 287 (2002): 1183.

37. John Bender, "From Theatre to Laboratory," *Journal of the American Medical Association* 287 (2002): 1179.

38. In 1745 the University of Pennsylvania established the first formal course in the study of anatomy in the United States. Sappol, *Traffic of Dead Bodies,* 60.

39. Sappol, *Traffic of Dead Bodies,* 60.

40. Sappol, *Traffic of Dead Bodies,* 2.

41. Dorothy Nelkin and Lori Andrews, "Do the Dead Have Interests? Policy Issues for Research after Life," *American Journal of Law and Medicine* 24, nos. 2–3 (1998): 261, 263.

42. Sappol, *Traffic of Dead Bodies,* 35–36.

43. *Mass. Gen. Laws* ch. 113, § 6. Dissection of bodies of executed murderers. The application of this statute is currently limited by the fact that Massachusetts does not impose a death penalty, although it would presumably apply to federal capital cases tried in Massachusetts.

44. Sappol, *Traffic of Dead Bodies,* 320.

45. Sappol, *Traffic of Dead Bodies,* 318.

46. The story of Burke and Hare is described in Suzanne M. Shultz, *Body Snatching: The Robbing of Graves for the Education of Physicians in Early Nineteenth Century America* (Jefferson, NC: McFarland, 1992), 69–70.

47. As well as giving rise to the neologism "to burke," meaning to suffocate. Tward and Patterson, "From Grave Robbing to Gifting," 1183; Sappol, *Traffic of Dead Bodies,* 118.

48. Sappol, *Traffic of Dead Bodies,* 115.

49. Horace Montgomery, "A Body Snatcher Sponsors Pennsylvania's Anatomy Act," *Journal of History and Medicine and Allied Sciences* 21 (1966): 376.

50. Sappol, *Traffic of Dead Bodies*, 4.

51. Sappol, *Traffic of Dead Bodies*, 101–2.

52. Sappol, *Traffic of Dead Bodies*, 4.

53. Kunal M. Parker, "State, Citizenship, and Territory: The Legal Construction of Immigrants in Antebellum Massachusetts," *Law and History Review* 19 (2001): 590–92. Sappol notes that the 1831 Massachusetts act applied only to Boston, the 1854 New York "Bone Bill" was limited to cities with populations over thirty thousand, and the 1867 Pennsylvania "Armstrong Act" was limited to Philadelphia and Pittsburgh. Sappol, *Traffic of Dead Bodies*, 123.

54. Sappol, *Traffic of Dead Bodies*, 123–24.

55. One side effect of these excess cadavers has been several scandals involving cadaver trafficking by officials at some of these institutions. For example, an article in the *Los Angeles Times* from March 2007 reported that criminal charges were filed against the director of the "willed body" program and another man who allegedly sold parts of donated bodies for a profit. According to authorities, they made more than a million dollars through their illegal activities. Charles Ornstein and Andrew Blankstein, "Two Men Charged in Sale of Donated Bodies," *Los Angeles Times,* 8 March 2007, 1.

56. Lindsey Gruson, "Signs of Traffic in Cadavers Seen, Raising Ethical Issues," *New York Times,* 25 September 1986, A14; Tward and Patterson, "From Grave Robbing to Gifting."

57. Jesse Dukeminier, Jr., "Supplying Organs for Transplantation," *Michigan Law Review* 68 (1970): 818.

58. Indeed, from the early days of transplants through to today, there has been a persistent and significant shortfall in the number of organs available to transplant. (In 2006 more than ninety-five thousand people were on a wait list awaiting an organ. On average eighteen people die each day because no organ is available for transplant.) See http://www.UNOS.org.

59. The UAGA was expansive in this area and provided for the donations of any human body or body part to: (1) any hospital, surgeon, or physician, for medical or dental education, research, advancement of medical or dental science, therapy, or transplantation; or (2) any accredited medical or dental school, college or university for education, research, advancement of medical or dental science, or therapy; or (3) any bank or storage facility, for medical or dental education, research, advancement of medical or dental science, therapy, or transplantation; or (4) any specified individual for therapy or transplantation needed by him. 1968 UAGA § 3.

60. 1987 UAGA Prefatory note, quoting Task Force on Organ Transplantation, "Organ Transplantation: Issues and Recommendations" (April 1986). The imbalance continues to worsen. As described in the 2006 UAGA Prefatory Note: "As of January, 2006 there were over 92,000 individuals on the waiting list for organ transplantation, and the list keeps growing. It is estimated that approximately 5,000 individuals join

the waiting list each year. . . . Every hour another person in the United States dies because of the lack of an organ to provide a life saving organ transplant." Revised UAGA (2006) Prefatory Note at http://www.law.upenn.edu/bll/ulc/uaga/2006final.htm.

61. 1987 UAGA § 5.

62. Erik S. Jaffe, "'She's Got Bette Davis['s] Eyes': Assessing the Nonconsensual Removal of Cadaver Organs under the Takings and Due Process Clauses," *Columbia Law Review* 90 (1990): 535.

63. *U.S. Code* 42 (2002) § 1320b-8.

64. 1987 UAGA § 4. Some state versions of presumed consent limit its application to certain body parts, such as corneas, pituitary glands, and other tissues. Other versions, including the UAGA, apply to all organs.

65. Michele Goodwin, *Black Markets: The Supply and Demand of Body Parts* (Cambridge: Cambridge University Press, 2006), 121.

66. Goodwin, *Black Markets*, 131–32.

67. *Brotherton v. Cleveland,* 173 F.3d 552 (6th Cir. 1999); *State v. Powell,* 497 So.2d 1188 (Fla. 1986), *cert. denied,* 481 U.S. 1059 (1987); *Georgia Lions Eye Bank v. Lavant,* 335 S.E.2d 127 (Ga. 1985); *Tillman v. Detroit Receiving Hosp.,* 360 N.W.2d 275 (Mich. Ct. App. 1984).

68. *Tillman,* 360 N.W. 2d 275, 277. The right to privacy is described in greater detail in chapter 4.

69. *Brotherton v. Cleveland,* 173 F.3d 552 (6th Cir. 1999).

70. Presumed consent laws have been implemented in Austria, Belgium, Czech Republic, Denmark, Finland, France, Greece, Hungary, Israel, Italy, Latvia, Luxembourg, Norway, Poland, Portugal, Singapore, Slovak Republic, Slovenia, Spain, Sweden, and Switzerland. See Marie-Andrée Jacob, "On Silencing and Slicing: Presumed Consent to Post-Mortem Organ 'Donation' in Diversified Societies," *Tulsa Journal of Comparative and International Law* 11 (Fall 2003): 239.

71. AP, "An Organ Donation Offer on Death Row Is Refused," *New York Times,* 9 September 1998, A23.

72. Laura-Hill M. Patton, "A Call for Common Sense: Organ Donation and the Executed Prisoner," *Virginia Journal of Social Policy and Law* 3 (1995): 387.

73. Donnye Perales, "Rethinking the Prohibition of Death Row Prisoners as Organ Donors: A Possible Life Line to Those on Organ Donor Waiting Lists," *St. Mary's Law Journal* 34 (2003): 687.

74. Perales, "Rethinking the Prohibition of Death Row Prisoners."

75. "Organ Sales 'Thriving' in China," *BBC News,* 27 September 2006. In China, for example, prisoners are routinely executed and their organs are reputedly sold by the government at large profits (reportedly more than 65 percent of Chinese organ donations come from death row prisoners). "China Admits to Death Row Organ Use," *BBC News,* 26 August 2009, available at: http://news.bbc.co.uk/2/hi/asia-pacific/8222732.stm.

76. AP, "Organ Donation Offer."

77. Brian Olshansky, MD, "For Whom Does the Bell Toll?" *Journal of Cardiovascular Electrophysiology* 12 (2001): 1002–3.

78. Joanna Bourke, *Fear: A Cultural History* (Berkeley, CA: Shoemaker and Hoard, 2006), 41–42.

79. Kenneth V. Iserson, *Death to Dust: What Happens to Dead Bodies* (Tucson, AZ: Galen Press, 1994), 13.

80. Marc Alexander, "'The Rigid Embrace of the Narrow House': Premature Burial and the Signs of Death," *Hastings Center Report* (June 1980): 25, 26.

81. Alexander, "'Rigid Embrace of the Narrow House.'"

82. Alexander, "'Rigid Embrace of the Narrow House.'"

83. Alexander, "'Rigid Embrace of the Narrow House,'" 31.

84. Iserson, *Death to Dust,* 19, n. 26. See also Twenty-Second World Medical Assembly, Sydney, Australia, 1968.

85. John P. Lizza, *Persons, Humanity, and the Definition of Death* (Baltimore: Johns Hopkins University Press, 2006), 7.

86. *State v. Schaffer,* 574 P. 2d 205 (1977); see also *People v. Eulo,* 472 N.E.2d 286 (N.Y. 1984).

87. This is the standard set out in the Uniform Determination of Death Act. As of 2009, this statute has been adopted in some form in more than forty states. This standard is different from a permanent vegetative state in that the brain of a person in a PVS still functions, albeit at a rudimentary state.

88. Lizza, *Persons, Humanity, and the Definition of Death,* 160.

89. Masahiro Morioka, "Reconsidering Brain Death: A Lesson from Japan's Fifteen Years of Experience," *Hastings Center Report,* July–August 2001, 41. Alex Martin, "Upper House Mulls Transplant Law," *Japan Times,* 27 June 2009. Editorial, "Vote a Step Forward for More Organ Donations," *Daily Yomiuri,* 19 June 2009.

90. Philip Brasor, "No Brains When It Comes Down to Transplants," *Japan Times,* 2 August 2009.

91. Megan Tench, "After Buddhist Dies, Legal Battle Continues: Kin, Hospital Split on When Death Occurs," *Boston Globe,* 3 December 2006, 1A; Megan Tench, "End-of-Life Lawsuit Outliving Its Subject: Kin to Appeal Dismissal Ruling," *Boston Globe,* 6 December 2006, 3B.

92. See Hall, Bobinski, and Orentlicher, *Bioethics and Public Health Law,* 336; *In re Welfare of Bowman,* 617 P.2d 731, 738 (Wash. 1980); and *In re Long Island Jewish Medical Center,* 641 N.Y.S.2d 989 (Sup. Ct. 1996).

93. *N.J.S.A.* 26:6A-5.

94. Tom Stacy, "Death, Privacy, and the Free Exercise of Religion," *Cornell Law Review* 77 (1992): 490.

95. *Brancato v. Moriscato,* 2003 WL 1090596 (Conn. Super. 2003). Compare with *In re Estate of Bonanno,* 745 N.Y.S.2d 813 (Sur. 2002) (allowing postmortem DNA testing of a blood sample retained by the coroner) and *In re Estate of Janis,* 600 N.Y.S.2d 416

(Sur. 1993) (refusing to order exhumation for DNA testing); Jesse Dukeminier et al., *Wills, Trusts, and Estates* (New York: Aspen, 2005), 101, n. 62.

96. See Kate Schuler, Note, "The Liberalization of Posthumous Paternity Testing —Expanding the Rights of Illegitimate Children," *Quinnipiac Probate Law Journal* 17 (2003): 150.

97. Dukeminier et al., *Wills, Trusts, and Estates,* 102.

98. Sharona Hoffman and Andrew P. Morriss, "New Reproductive Technologies and the Inheritance Rights of Children: Currents in Contemporary Ethics," *Journal of Law, Medicine, and Ethics* 31 (2003): 721. Many storage facilities, however, have policies to destroy embryos after a certain period of time.

99. Kristine S. Knaplund, "Postmortem Conception and a Father's Last Will," *Arizona Law Review* 46 (2004): 91.

100. John A. Robertson, "Emerging Paradigms in Bioethics," *Indiana Law Journal* 69 (1994): 1027. In the recent case of *Estate of Kievernagel v. Kievernagel,* a court denied a woman the use of her husband's frozen sperm to conceive after her husband's death where the husband's agreement with the company storing the sperm was that the sperm was to be destroyed after his death. The court concluded that only the husband had an ownership interest in his sperm and thus only he had decision-making authority as to the use of his sperm. By signing an agreement with the company that the sperm should be destroyed after his death, there could be no other option but to carry out his wishes. 83 Cal. Rptr. 3d 311 (Ct. App. 2008).

101. Radhika Rao, "Equal Liberty: Assisted Reproductive Technology and Reproductive Equality," *George Washington Law Review* 76 (2008): 1457.

102. *Hecht v. Superior Court,* 20 Cal. Rptr. 2d 275 (Ct. App. 1993).

103. *Hecht,* 20 Cal. Rptr. 2d 275.

104. 59 Cal. Rptr. 2d 222 at 226 (Ct. App. 1996). This special treatment of reproductive matter has also been employed with respect to the disposition of embryos in connection with divorce. In *Davis v. Davis,* 842 S.W.2d 588, 597 (Tenn. 1992), the Tennessee Supreme Court described the nature of the interest as follows: "We conclude that preembryos are not, strictly speaking, either 'persons' or 'property,' but occupy an interim category that entitles them to special respect because of their potential for human life. It follows that any interest that Mary Sue Davis and Junior Davis [the genetic donors] have in the preembryos in this case is not a true property interest. However, they do have an interest in the nature of ownership, to the extent that they have decision-making authority concerning disposition of the preembryos, within the scope of policy set by law."

105. *Davis,* 842 S.W.2d 588, 597.

106. William H. Danne, Jr., "Legal Status of Posthumously Conceived Children of the Decedent," 17 A.L.R. 6th 593 (2006).

107. *Finely v. Astrue,* 270 S.W.3d 849 (Ark. 2007); *Khabbaz v. Commissioner, Social Security Administration,* 930 A.2d 1180 (N.H. 2007).

108. Section 4(b) provides: "An individual who dies before implantation of an em-

bryo, or before a child is conceived other than through sexual intercourse, using the individual's egg or sperm, is not a parent of the resulting child."

109. See *Woodward v. Commissioner of Social Security,* 760 N.E.2d 257 (Mass. 2002); and *In re Estate of Kolacy,* 753 A.2d 1257 (N.J. Super. Ct. Ch. Div. 2000). This is also the position of the Restatement Third, Property § 2.05, Comment 1. But see, e.g., *Khabbaz,* 930 A.2d 1180 (holding that statutes governing artificial insemination did not render child eligible to inherit from father).

110. UPA (rev. 2002), sec. 707.

111. R. D. Orr and M. Siegler, "Is Posthumous Semen Retrieval Ethically Permissible?" *Journal of Medical Ethics* 28 (2002): 299.

112. Kathryn D. Katz, "Parenthood from the Grave: Protocols for Retrieving and Utilizing Gametes from the Dead or Dying," *University of Chicago Legal Forum* (2006): 289.

113. Katz, "Parenthood from the Grave," 300.

114. Katz, "Parenthood from the Grave," 291. There have been at least eleven reported cases of irretrievably brain-damaged women whose lives were prolonged for the benefit of a developing fetus.

115. Daniel Sperling, "Maternal Brain Death," *American Journal of Law and Medicine* 30 (2004): 453.

116. See *Cruzan v. Director, Mo. Dept. of Health,* 497 U.S. 261 (1990).

117. Katz, "Parenthood from the Grave," 291, citing Bretton H. Horner, "A Survey of Living Wills," *North Dakota Law Review* 74 (1998): 233.

118. *Univ. Health Servs., Inc. v. Piazzi,* No. CV86-RCCV-464 (Ga. Super. Ct., 1986).

119. Arthur Rowe, PhD, of the New York University School of Medicine, quoted in Iserson, *Death to Dust,* 290.

120. Robert C. W. Ettinger, *The Prospect of Immortality* (New York: Doubleday, 1964).

121. Ettinger, *Prospect of Immortality,* 1.

122. This occurred in 1967. Iserson, *Death to Dust,* 289.

123. David M. Baker, Comment, "Cryonic Preservation of Human Bodies—A Call for Legislative Action," *Dickinson Law Review* 98 (1994): 686 and nn. 86–91.

124. "A person must not offer for sale or sell any arrangement for the preservation or storage of human remains based on cryonics, irradiation or any other means of preservation or storage, by whatever name called, that is offered or sold on the expectation of the resuscitation of human remains at a future time." Cemetery and Funeral Services Act R.S.B.C. 1996, c. 45, s. 57.

125. Ariane Bernard, "Son Ordered to Bury or Cremate His Frozen Parents," *New York Times,* 11 January 2006, A17.

126. C.G.S.A. § 45a-318.

127. 63 Op. Att'y Gen. Cal. 879, 888 (1980).

128. The lawsuit was brought under the pseudonym John Roe. This case is dis-

cussed in Adam J. Perlin, "To Die in Order to Live: The Need for Legislation Governing Post-Mortem Cryonic Suspension," *Southwestern University Law Review* 36 (2007): 46–47.

129. *Alcor Life Extension Foundation, Inc. v. Mitchell,* 9 Cal. Rptr. 2d 572 (Ct. App. 1992).

130. See   http://www.alcor.org/printable.cgi?fname=Library/html/legislation. html.

131. Richard Sandomir, "Note Dated 2000 Says Williams Wanted His Remains Frozen," *New York Times,* 26 July 2002, D1.

132. In the words of two early cryonicists: "He is not completely dead, since most of the cells are still living—this is what cryonic suspension is all about." Curtis Henderson and Robert C. W. Ettinger, "Cryonic Suspension and the Law," *UCLA Law Review* 15 (1967–68): 415.

133. See http://www.alcor.org/AboutCryonics/index.html.

134. Antonio Regalado, "A Cold Calculus Leads Cryonauts to Put Assets on Ice," *Wall Street Journal,* 21 January 2006, A1.

135. Regalado, "Cold Calculus."

Chapter 2: Controlling Property (Part 1)

1. Although some of these advantages can also be obtained through lifetime gifts, the natural desire to hold onto power and property as long as possible (as well as the specter of King Lear) makes lifetime gifts far less desirable than transfers at death— when the owner's separation from his or her property is unavoidable.

2. *Hodel v. Irving,* 481 U.S. 704, 716 (1987).

3. Adam Hirsch, "American History of Inheritance Law" (Working paper, FSU College of Law, Public Law Research Paper no. 258, 2007).

4. Thomas Glyn Watkin, *An Historical Introduction to Modern Civil Law* (Hampshire, UK: Ashgate 1999), 192–218.

5. Mathias Reimann and Reinhard Zimmermann, *The Oxford Handbook of Comparative Law* (New York: Oxford University Press, 2007), 1085; D. J. Hayton, *European Succession Laws,* European Practice Library (London: Chancery Law, 1991).

6. *Fischer v. Heckerman,* 772 S.W.2d 642, 645 (Ky. Ct. App. 1989).

7. Family maintenance statutes were first enacted in New Zealand in 1900. Testator's Family Maintenance Act of 1900, *N.Z. Stat.* No. 20 (1900). This served as the basis for the current testate succession laws in Australia, several Canadian provinces, and England. Ralph C. Brashier, "Disinheritance and the Modern Family," *Case Western Reserve Law Review* 45 (1994): 83, 121, n. 125. England adopted its first family maintenance statute in 1938. Inheritance (Family Provision) Act 1938, 1 & 2 Geo. 6, ch. 45 (1938) (Eng.). For a detailed discussion of English law, see Alexandra Mason and Marian Conroy, *Spencer Maurice's Family Provision on Death,* 7th ed. (London: Sweet and Maxwell, 1994).

8. Inheritance (Provisions for Family and Dependants) Act, ch. 63 § 1(1) (1975) (Eng.). An earlier version of this statute was enacted in 1938.

9. Inheritance (Provisions for Family and Dependants) Act, ch. 63 § 3. British Columbia also has a family maintenance statute. However, unlike the statute in England, which provides support for certain dependents, the British Columbia statute provides protections for family members regardless of need. Ronald Chester, "Disinheritance and the American Child: An Alternative from British Columbia," *Utah Law Review* 1998 (1998): 1.

10. *Bosch v. Perpetual Trustee Co., Ltd.*, [1938] A.C.463 at 478–479 (P.C.) (appeal taken from N.S.W.).

11. See Ralph C. Brashier, "Protecting the Child from Disinheritance: Must Louisiana Stand Alone?" *Louisiana Law Review* 57 (1996): 1, 5, n. 23.

12. There are generally two situations in which parents can inherit significant assets from their children. The first is when a child has no assets during life but on death his or her estate has value as a result of a wrongful death claim. The second situation is when a child accumulates substantial earnings or receives a large personal injury or wrongful death award during the child's lifetime (typically for a parent's death). Paula A. Monopoli, "Deadbeat Dads: Should Support and Inheritance Be Linked?" *University of Miami Law Review* 49 (1994): 257.

13. *Herring v. Moore*, 561 S.W.2d 95, 96–97 (Ky. Ct. App. 1977). Cited in Brashier, "Protecting the Child from Disinheritance," 11.

14. Brashier, "Protecting the Child from Disinheritance," 11.

15. See *L.M. v. R.L.R.*, 451 Mass. 682 (2008).

16. *Benson ex rel. Patterson v. Patterson*, 830 A.2d 966 (Pa. 2003).

17. Brashier, "Protecting the Child from Disinheritance"; Chester, "Disinheritance and the American Child."

18. Texas is the only other state that has ever tried forced heirship, a remnant of the state's Spanish law history. After Texas entered the Union in 1846, the common law influence in this area became stronger and more expansive. Texas abolished forced heirship altogether in 1856. See Joseph Dainow, "The Early Sources of Forced Heirship: Its History in Texas and Louisiana," *Louisiana Law Review* 4 (1941): 42, 56–57.

19. See *La. Civ. Code Ann.* art. 1493 (West 1987). See also Mary Ann Glendon, "Family Law Reform in the 1980's," *Louisiana Law Review* 44 (1984): 1553, 1570–73.

20. See *La. Civ. Code Ann.* art. 1495 (providing that donor may disinherit heirs for just cause).

21. The language that was originally adopted provided forced heir status for those children under the age of twenty-three or those who were interdicted or subject to interdiction. 1989 *La. Acts* 788. The language was changed in 1990 *La. Acts* 147 to the language in the main text to avoid ambiguity by substituting the language of the code sections regarding interdiction.

22. See generally Katherine S. Spaht et al., "The New Forced Heirship Legislation: A Regrettable 'Revolution,'" *Louisiana Law Review* 50 (1990): 409.

23. There were some bumps on the road in the elimination of forced heirship because after it was repealed by legislature, the Louisiana Supreme Court declared the repeal to be unconstitutional under the state constitution in 1993. The court's holding

of unconstitutionality was announced in the companion cases of *Succession of Lauga,* 624 So. 2d 1156 (La. 1993), and *Succession of Terry,* 624 So. 2d 1201 (La. 1993). Louisiana subsequently amended its constitution to allow for the limitation of forced heirship, and the statutory provision was reenacted in 1996. Article XII, § 5 of the 1995 Louisiana Constitution and *La. Civ. Code* art. 1493, 1495, and 1496 (1996).

24. I.R.C. § 102 (1986). Assuming they are subject to tax at the highest rates.

25. This is because the recipient of a gift takes the same basis in the property that the donor has. I.R.C. § 1015 (1997).

26. Thus, if the recipient sells the property the next day for a hundred thousand dollars, he or she pays no taxes on that transfer. I.R.C. § 1016 (1984).

27. Edward N. Wolff, "Recent Trends in Household Wealth in the United States: Rising Debt and the Middle Class Squeeze" (Bard College, Levy Economics Institute, working paper no. 502, 2007).

28. James Repetti, "Democracy, Taxes and Wealth," *New York University Law Review* 76 (2001): 825, 831.

29. Repetti, "Democracy, Taxes and Wealth," 827.

30. William H. Gates and Chuck Collins, *Wealth and Our Commonwealth* (Boston: Beacon Press, 2002), 17.

31. As the great nineteenth-century commentator Alexis de Tocqueville said: "The American experiment presupposes a rejection of inherited privilege." Quoted in Collins and Gates, *Wealth and Our Commonwealth,* 27.

32. James L. Huston, *Securing the Fruits of Labor: The American Concept of Wealth Distribution, 1765–1900* (Baton Rouge: Louisiana State University Press, 1998), 385, citing Lee Soltow, *Men and Wealth in the United States, 1850–1870* (New Haven: Yale University Press, 1975), 113.

33. Joseph Frazier Wall, ed., *The Andrew Carnegie Reader* (Pittsburgh: University of Pittsburgh Press, 1992), x.

34. "The Gospel of Wealth," in Wall, ed., *Andrew Carnegie Reader,* 134–35.

35. "Gospel of Wealth," 136.

36. See James Repetti, Paul McDaniel, and Paul Caron, *Federal Wealth Transfer Taxation,* 5th ed. (New York: Foundation Press, 2003), 2–12.

37. Caole Shammas, Marylynn Salmon, and Michel Dahlin, *Inheritance in America: From Colonial Times to the Present* (Galveston, TX: Frontier Press, 1997).

38. Collins and Gates, *Wealth and Our Commonwealth,* 15; Edward N. Wolff, *Top Heavy: A Study of the Increasing Inequality of Wealth in America* (New York: Twentieth Century Fund Press, 1995), 8–13.

39. Wolff, "Recent Trends in Household Wealth." Moreover, there is evidence to suggest that not only are the rich getting richer, they are doing so at an ever increasing speed. Thus, while the average wealth of the top 1 percent grew by 3 percent between 2001 and 2004 (from $12.5 million to $14.8 million), the average wealth of the middle 20 percent of households grew less than 1 percent in that same period (from $80,000 in 2001 to $81,900 in 2004).

40. Lawrence Mishel, Jared Bernstein, and Sylvia Allegretto, *The State of Working America, 2004–2005* (Ithaca, NY: Cornell University Press, 2005), 256.

41. Paul L. Menchik and Nancy Ammon Jianakoplos, "Black-White Wealth Inequality: Is Inheritance the Reason?" *Economic Inquiry* 35 (1997): 428.

42. "Inheritances Perpetuate a Racial Divide," *Boston Sunday Globe,* 14 December 1997, 1.

43. Robert B. Avery and Michael S. Rendell, "Lifetime Inheritances of Three Generations of Whites and Blacks," *American Journal of Sociology* 107 (2002): 1300–1346.

44. Avery and Rendell, "Lifetime Inheritances," 1335.

45. Lily L. Batchelder, "Taxing Privilege More Effectively: Replacing the Estate Tax with an Inheritance Tax," *Law and Economics,* Research Paper Series, working paper no. 07-25 (July 2007), 51.

46. Reuven Avi-Yonah, "Why Tax the Rich: Efficiency, Equity, and Progressive Taxation," *Yale Law Journal* 111 (2002): 1391, 1406.

47. Repetti, "Democracy, Taxes and Wealth," 850.

48. Repetti, "Democracy, Taxes and Wealth," 850.

49. Charitable giving is discussed in greater detail in chapter 3.

50. Although restrictions can also be imposed through title, courts have been less accepting of these limitations. See *Drace v. Klinedinst,* 118 A. 907, 908 (Pa. 1922), in which the court said: "The policy of the law is to keep the alienation of land free from embarrassing impediments, and it endeavors to strip devises and grants of restrictive conditions, tending to fetter free disposition." See also *Cast v. Nat'l Bank of Commerce Trust and Sav. Ass'n of Lincoln,* 183 N.W.2d 485, 489 (Neb. 1971), in which the court stated: "It seems to us that a condition attached to a fee simple title which has for its purpose the satisfaction of a whimsical obsession or an expression of testator's vanity ought not be permitted as a fettering of a fee simple title. Such a condition is unreasonable in that fee titles to real estate are not proper places for trivial conditions evidencing personal whimsy."

51. D. J. Hayton, *The Law of Trusts,* 3rd ed. (London: Sweet and Maxwell, 1998), 93–96.

52. Frachter, 1 Scott on Trusts § 337, 4th ed. (Boston: Little, Brown, 1987), 436.

53. Frachter, 1 Scott on Trusts, § 1, at 2.

54. In one case familiar to every law student, an uncle promised his nephew five thousand dollars if he would refrain from drinking, using tobacco, swearing, and playing cards until his twenty-first birthday. The court found that it was a valid contract and that the nephew, having held to his side of the bargain, was entitled to receive the five thousand dollars from his uncle's estate. *Hamer v. Sidway,* 27 N.E. 256 (1891).

55. *In re Rolosm's Will,* 155 N.Y.S. 2d 140, 146–47 (N.Y.Sur. 1956).

56. Jeffrey G. Sherman, "Posthumous Meddling: An Instrumental Theory of Testamentary Restraints on Conjugal and Religious Choices," *University of Illinois Law Review* 1999 (1999): 1273, 1280, n.34.

57. *Tunstall v. Wells,* 50 Cal. Rptr. 3d 468, 565 (Cal. Ct. App. 2006).

58. *Loving v. Virginia,* 388 U.S. 1, 12 (1967).

59. *Commonwealth v. Stauffer,* 10 Pa. 350 (1849). Cited in Sherman, "Posthumous Meddling." Although courts also support wives' conditioning their husband's bequest on the husband not remarrying, the opportunity for women to impose these

conditions is far more limited, since women historically control less property than their husbands and also tend to live longer than their husbands.

60. *Shapira v. Union Nat. Bank,* 315 N.E.2d 825 (Ohio Ct. Com. Pl. 1974). Cited in Jesse Dukeminier et al., *Wills, Trusts, and Estates,* 7th ed. (New York: Aspen, 2005).

61. *In re Estate of Keffalas,* 233 A.2d 248 (Pa. 1967). Cited in Sherman, "Posthumous Meddling."

62. For example, in the Keffalas case, where the children were required to marry spouses "of true Greek blood and descent and of Orthodox religion"—the court refused to apply the limitation to those children who were already married to other spouses and would therefore have been required to divorce and remarry someone of the appropriate background in order to inherit. *In re Estate of Keffalas,* 233 A.2d 248.

63. *Hall v. Eaton,* 631 N.E.2d 805, 808 (Ill. App. Ct. 1994).

64. *Chamberlian v. Van Horn,* 141 N.E. 111 (Mass. 1923).

65. *Delaware Trust Co. v. Fitzmaurice,* 31 A.2d 383 (Del. Ch. 1943); aff'd in part and rev'd in part on other grounds sub nom, *Crumlish v. Delaware Trust Co.,* 38 A.2d 463 (Del. Super. Ct. 1944).

66. *In re Lanning's Estate,* 339 A.2d 520 (Pa. 1975).

67. *In re Paulson's Will,* 107 N.W. 484 (Wis. 1906). Cited in Sherman, "Posthumous Meddling."

68. *U.S. Nat. Bank of Portland v. Snodgrass,* 275 P.2d 860 (Or. 1954). Cited in E. LeFevre, *Validity of Provisition of Will or Deed Prohibiting, Penalizing, or Requiring Marriage to One of a Particular Religious Faith,* 50 A.L.R.2d 740 (1956).

69. Sherman, "Posthumous Meddling."

70. Duke of Norfolk's Case (1682), 22 Eng. Rep. 931.

71. Mark Reutlinger describes this reference as follows: "[This] reflects the Rule's status as more than just another legal doctrine. It is *the* Rule, more feared, criticized, misunderstood, and ironically ruthlessly applied, than any other in the law of property." Reutlinger, *Wills, Trusts and Estates,* 2nd ed. (New York: Aspen, 1998), 188–89.

72. Lewis M. Simes, *Public Policy and the Dead Hand* (Ann Arbor: University of Michigan Law School, 1955), 59.

73. Indeed, the Rule has even crept into popular culture: violation of the Rule provided the denouement in the 1981 feature film *Body Heat.*

74. John Chipman Gray, *The Rule against Perpetuities,* 4th ed. (Frederick, MD: Beard Books, 1942), 191.

75. "To my son for life, then to his widow for her life, and at her death to his children then surviving." See *Pound v. Shorter,* 377 S.E.2d 854 (Ga. 1989). The final gift to the grandchildren is void because the son might marry someone not alive when the testator died. The "widow" could not serve as the validating life. Although its most common application is to spouses, the principle applies to anyone identified by description rather than by name.

76. *Lucas v. Hamm,* 364 P.2d 685 (Cal. 1961).

77. Max M. Schanzenbach and Robert H. Sitkoff, "Perpetuities or Taxes? Explaining the Rise of the Perpetual Trust," *Cardozo Law Review* 27 (2006): 2465, 2474.

78. For example, if the beneficiary had a right to income only for his or her life or was a discretionary beneficiary, such that he or she could not demand a certain amount, then the property would not be subject to tax in his or her estate. Ray Madoff, Cornelia Tenney, and Martin Hall, *Practical Guide to Estate Planning* (Chicago: CCH, 2007), § 6.62.

79. Regis Campfield, Martin Dickinson, and William Turnier, *Taxation of Estates, Gifts and Trusts,* 23rd ed. (St. Paul, MN: Thomson West, 1997), 727.

80. *Generation-Skipping Transfer Tax: Hearing before the H. Comm. on Ways and Means,* 98th Cong., 335, 336 (1984) (testimony of Raymond Young). Young then observed that such a trust could "last within the period of the rule against perpetuities." Schanzenbach and Sitkoff, "Perpetuities or Taxes?" 2465, 2477.

81. See Dukeminier, *Wills, Trusts, and Estates,* 714 (reproducing a Wells Fargo advertisement touting South Dakota as a "place where there is no rule against perpetuities" as well as "no fiduciary income tax"). Robert H. Sitkoff and Max M. Schanzenbach, "Jurisdictional Competition for Trust Funds: An Empirical Analysis of Perpetuities and Taxes," *Yale Law Journal* 115 (2005): 356, 356, n. 5.

82. This is discussed in Schanzenbach and Sitkoff, "Perpetuities or Taxes?" 2474.

83. Sitkoff and Schanzenbach, "Jurisdictional Competition for Trust Funds," 353.

84. John Budihas, "A Trust to Help Clients Create a Dynasty (Advanced Markets)," *The National Underwriter Company National Underwriter Life and Health Financial-Services Edition,* 10 November 2003.

85. Madoff, Tenney, and Hall, *Practical Guide to Estate Planning,* § 9.04 (by Georgiana Slade).

86. Madoff, Tenney, and Hall, *Practical Guide to Estate Planning,* § 9.04[B][2](by Georgiana Slade).

87. Catherine M. Allchin, "In Some Trusts, the Heirs Must Work for the Money," *New York Times,* 29 January 2006.

Chapter 3: Controlling Property (Part 2)

1. Paul Schervish and John Havens, "Gifts and Bequests: Family or Philanthropic Organizations?" in *Death and Dollars: The Role of Gifts and Bequests in America,* ed. Alicia H. Munnell and Annika Sunden (Washington, DC: Brookings Institute Press, 2003).

2. Frederic Golden, "The Worst and the Brightest," *Time,* 16 October 2000.

3. Golden, "Worst and Brightest."

4. Restatements are distillations of common law prepared by the American Law Institute (ALI), a prestigious organization comprising judges, professors, and lawyers. The ALI's aim is to restate existing common law into a series of principles or rules.

5. Restatement (Second) of Trusts, § 368 (1959).

6. As an example of the difficulty of the English language that Shaw thought to address, consider the following problem: the word "through" is composed of three basic sounds (th, r, ough) but has seven letters. The first sound can only be writ-

ten with two letters, and the last sound is written with four letters. Alternatively, "through" could be written as "thru," "thrue," or "throo," with the same pronunciation of the last sound. Remove the first two letters of "through," and logically you should end up with a word that rhymes with "through." Instead, you get the word "rough," which alternately could have been spelled "ruff."

7. *In re Shaw,* [1957] 1 All. E.R. 745, 759 (Ch.).

8. *Jackson v. Phillips,* 96 Mass. (14 Allen) 539, 570 (1867). In rejecting the charitable nature, the court stated: "Whether such an alteration of the existing laws and frame of government would be wise and desirable is a question upon which we cannot, sitting in a judicial capacity, properly express any opinion. Our duty is limited to expounding the laws as they stand. And those laws do not recognize the purpose of overthrowing or changing them, in whole or in part, as a charitable use. This bequest therefore, not being for a charitable purpose, nor for the benefit of any particular persons, and being unrestricted in point of time, is inoperative and void." Interestingly, a bequest in the same will "for the benefit of fugitive slaves who may escape from the slaveholding states of this infamous Union from time to time," was found to be charitable.

9. *Register of Wills for Baltimore City v. Cook,* 216 A.2d 542 (Md. 1966).

10. *Marsh v. Frost Nat'l Bank,* 129 S.W.3d 174, 178 (Tex. App. 2004). To address the problem of management over time, Walker provided that when the fund reached fifteen million dollars, it would be turned over to the secretary of the treasury for management by the federal government, and he directed that Congress would make the final rules as to how the money would be distributed. The only rule Walker put in place was that "no one shall be denied their share because of race, religion, marital status, sexual preference, or the amount of their wealth or lack thereof."

11. *Marsh,* 129 S.W.3d 174, 178.

12. Lewis M. Simes, *Public Policy and the Dead Hand* (Ann Arbor: University of Michigan Law School, 1955), 118.

13. In order for a private trust to be valid, it must have ascertainable beneficiaries and the life of the trust must be limited to the time period authorized by the Rule against Perpetuities.

14. Kymson F. DesJardins, "Mortmain Statutes: Questions of Constitutionality," *Notre Dome Law Review* 52 (1977): 638, 639.

15. Lawrence Friedman, *A History of American Law* (New York: Simon and Schuster, 2005), 185.

16. *Ga. Code Ann.* § 53-2-10 (2007).

17. "In the early nineteenth century, charity was associated with privilege, with the dead hand, and with massive wealth held in perpetuity. None of these was particularly popular." Friedman, *History of American Law,* 185.

18. Elizabeth Fleet, "Madison's 'Detached Memoranda,'" *William and Mary Quarterly,* 3rd ser., 3 (1946): 534–68 [excerpted language is from 556–57, estimated to have been written by Madison between 1817 and 1832].

19. "The greater became the Church holdings, and they were usually of the best land in a given community, the less land was left for the laity to own, and the fewer

were the chances that the very small incipient middle class would get a foothold." Wilfred Hardy Callcott, *Church and State in Mexico, 1822–1857* (New York: Octogon Books, 1965), 14.

20. Evelyn Brody, "Charitable Endowments and the Democratization of Dynasty," *Arizona Law Review* 39 (1977): 873, 914.

21. *Philadelphia Baptist Ass'n v. Hart's Executors,* 17 U.S. (4 Wheat.) 1 (1819). Discussed in Howard Miller, *The Legal Foundations of American Pilanthropy, 1776–1844* (Ann Arbor, MI: Cushing-Malloy, 1961), 21–23; and Marion R. Fremont-Smith, *Governing Nonprofit Organizations: Federal and State Law and Regulations* (Cambridge, MA: Harvard University Press, 2004), 45.

22. "The *Hart* case was followed in Virginia, Maryland, the District of Columbia, and West Virginia for nearly one hundred years; and it influenced the development of charitable trusts in New York, Michigan, Wisconsin, and Minnesota. It had this effect despite the fact that twenty-five years later the Supreme Court reversed itself in *Vidal v. Girard's Executors,* holding that charitable trusts should be afforded recognition in the United States regardless of statutes abolishing English law." Fremont-Smith, *Governing Nonprofit Organizations,* 45.

23. *Bascom v. Albertson,* 34 N.Y. 584, 614–15 (1866), cited in Fremont-Smith, *Governing Nonprofit Organizations,* 46.

24. Samuel Tilden was the Al Gore of his day. He was the democratic candidate of 1876, the most controversial presidential election of the nineteenth century. In 1876 Tilden won the popular vote by more than 250,000 votes, but after months of dispute, the election was ultimately handed over to the Republican candidate, Rutherford B. Hayes.

25. Friedman, *History of American Law,* 318; *Tilden v. Green,* 28 N.E. 880 (1891). The case is discussed and criticized in a contemporaneous law review article: Manes B. Ames, "The Failure of the Tilden Trust," *Harvard Law Review* 5 (1982): 389.

26. Tilden Acts of 1893, ch. 701, codified at N.Y. Real Prop., § 113; N.Y. Pers. Prop., § 12. Discussed in Fremont-Smith, *Governing Nonprofit Organizations,* 46–47.

27. *Vidal v. Girard's Ex'rs,* 43 U.S. (2 How.) 127 (1844).

28. Fremont-Smith, *Governing Nonprofit Organizations,* 47.

29. Miller, *Legal Foundations,* 40–41.

30. See note 23, above.

31. Charities Act, 2006, c. 50, §§ 2–3 (Eng.). Tiffany Keb, "Redefining What It Means to Be Charitable: Raising the Bar with a Public Interest Requirement," *Oregon Law Review* 86 (2007): 865.

32. George W. Keeton and Lionel Astor Sheridan, *The Modern Law of Charities* (Belfast: Northern Ireland Quarterly, 1971), as cited in Frances Howell Rudko, "The Cy Pres Doctrine in the United States: From Extreme Reluctance to Affirmative Action," *Cleveland State Law Review* 46 (1998): 471.

33. Although the writing in wills is often spare, Bacon's will is unusually personal in explaining his motivation: "I am moved to make this bequest . . . by my gratitude to and love of the people of the City of Macon from whom through a long lifetime I

have received so much of personal kindness and so much of public honor; and especially as a memorial to my ever lamented and only sons, Lamar Bacon who died on the 21st day of December 1884 and Augustus Octavius Bacon, Jr. who died on the 27th day of the same year. And I conjure all of my descendants to the remotest generation as they shall honor my memory and respect my wishes to see to it that this property is cared for, protected and preserved forever for the uses and purposes herein indicated."

34. *Evans v. Newton,* 382 U.S. 296 (1966).

35. Evelyn Brody, "Whose Public? Parochialism and Paternalism in State Charity Law Enforcement," *Indiana Law Journal* 79 (2004): 937, 985.

36. Bob Fernandez, "Hershey Trust's CEO Will Retire," *Philadelphia Inquirer,* 10 April 2008.

37. Steven Pearlstein, "A Bitter Feud Erupts over Hershey Plant: Plan to Sell Candy Empire Divides a Company Town," *Washington Post,* 2 September 2002, A1, as cited in Brody, "Whose Public?" 989.

38. Brody, "Whose Public?" 989.

39. Lewis M. Simes, *Public Policy and the Dead Hand* (Ann Arbor: University of Michigan Law School, 1955), 111.

40. Brody, "Charitable Endowments," 898–99.

41. Brody, "Charitable Endowments," 898–99.

42. Brody, "Charitable Endowments," 919.

43. Martin Morse Wooster, "The Greatest Twentieth Century Donor You've Never Heard Of," *On Line Opinion,* 2 August 2006. (I notice, as I write this book, that although Microsoft Word easily recognizes the names of the other well-known philanthropists, it suggests alternate spellings for Julius Rosenwald.)

44. Julius Rosenwald, "Principles of Public Giving," *Atlantic Monthly,* May 1929, 143.

45. Renee A. Irvin, "Endowments: Stable Largesse or Distortion of the Polity," *Public Administrative Review* 67 (2007): 445.

46. Buffet gave them ten years to disburse money from transfers made on Buffet's death.

47. Neil Brooks, "Review of Surrey and McDaniel (1985)," *Canadian Tax Journal* 34 (1986): 681–94.

48. *Report of the Senate Budget Committee, First Concurrent Resolution on the Budget—Fiscal Year 1977,* S. Rep. No. 94-731, 94th Cong., 2nd Sess., 8 (1976), cited in Paul R. McDaniel, James R. Repetti, and Paul L. Caron, *Federal Wealth Transfer Taxation,* 5th ed. (New York: Foundation Press, 2003), 598. Since 1974 (and pursuant to federal law) each administration has published a list of tax expenditures as part of its annual budget submission. However, beginning in 2003, with the quasi-repeal of the estate and gift tax, administrations stopped calculating tax expenditures in connection with estates and gifts. Leonard E. Burman, "Is the Tax Expenditure Concept Still Relevant?" *National Tax Journal* 56 (2003): 613.

49. Saul Levmore, "Taxes as Ballots," *University of Chicago Law Review* 65 (1998): 387, 405.

50. Stephanie Strom, "Big Gifts, Tax Breaks and a Debate on Charity," *New York Times,* 6 September 2007.

51. *Giving USA* (Glenview, IL: Giving USA Foundation, 2007), 74–75.

52. Miranda Perry Fleischer, "*Charitable Contributions in an Ideal Estate Tax,*" *Tax Law Review* 60 (2007): 263, 303.

53. Rob Reich, "A Failure of Philanthropy: American Charity Shortchanges the Poor, and Public Policy Is Partly to Blame," *Stanford Social Innovation Review* (Winter 2005): 24–33.

54. Strom, "Big Gifts."

55. Restatement of Trusts §§ 124 cmt. F (1935); Restatement (Second) of Trusts §§ 123 cmt. f, cmt. a, and cmt. b (1959).

56. "Leona Helmsley's Dog Loses All but $2 Million," *New York Times,* 17 June 2008.

57. Adam J. Hirsh, "Bequests for a Purpose: A Unified Theory," *Washington and Lee Law Review* 56 (1999): 33, 73.

58. Restatement (Second) of Trusts, § 124 cmt. g (1959).

59. *Rosser v. Prem,* 449 A.2d 461, 471 (Md. Ct. Spec. App. 1982).

60. *Fidelity Title & Trust Co. v. Clyde,* 121 A.2d 625, 629 (Conn. 1956).

61. Restatement (Second) of Trusts, § 124 cmt. g (1959).

62. Hirsch, "Bequests for a Purpose," 76, n. 157.

63. Hirsch, "Bequests for a Purpose," 76, n. 157.

Chapter 4: Controlling Reputation

1. Ruth Bordin, *Frances Willard: A Biography* (Chapel Hill: University of North Carolina Press, 1986), 3–6.

2. Shakespeare, *Othello,* 2.3.246–48.

3. Barr McClellan, *Blood, Money and Power: How L.B.J. Killed J.F.K.* (New York: Hannover House, 2003). The television documentary, *The Guilty Men,* aired on the History Channel in November 2003.

4. Bruce Weber, "Moyers and Others Want History Channel Inquiry over Film That Accuses Johnson," *New York Times,* 5 February 2004.

5. Dan Dobbs, *The Law of Torts* (St. Paul, MN: West Group, 2000), 1117. Although both libel and slander apply to false communications, libel applies to written communications, and slander applies to oral communications.

6. *New York Times Co. v. Sullivan,* 376 U.S. 254 (1964).

7. *Kono v. Meeker,* No. 06-1554, slip op. at 2 (Iowa Ct. App. 12 Dec. 2007).

8. *Gugliuzza v. K.C.M.C., Inc.,* 606 So.2d 790, 791 (La. 1992).

9. *Johnson v. KTBS, Inc.,* 899 So.2d 329 (La. Ct. App. 2004).

10. *Johnson,* 899 So.2d 329.

11. Richard P. Mandel and Renee Hobbs, "The Right to a Reputation after Death," *Communications and the Law* 13 (March 1991): 29–31.

12. Samuel D. Warren and Louis D. Brandeis, "The Right to Privacy," *Harvard Law Review* 4 (1890): 193. Though written as if it were describing an existing phenomenon, the article is widely regarded as having given birth to the right of privacy. See M. C. Slough, *Privacy, Freedom and Responsibility* (Springfield, IL: Charles C. Thomas, 1969), 27–42.

13. Warren and Brandeis, "Right to Privacy," 193.

14. Barbara Singer, "The Right of Publicity: Star Vehicle or Shooting Star?" *Cardozo Arts and Entertainment Law Journal* 10 (1992): 1, 6. It is reported that Brandeis and Warren first became interested in the problem of privacy and decided to write their article as a direct result of the Boston newspapers' practices of reporting on the affairs of Warren and his wife in lurid detail. Melville Nimmer, "The Right of Publicity," *Law and Contemporary Problems* 19 (1954): 203, 206.

15. Warren and Brandeis, "Right to Privacy," 195. The significant technological change involved the advancements in photography. As the authors later explain: "While, for instance, the state of the photographic art was such that one's picture could seldom be taken without his consciously 'sitting' for the purpose, the law of contract or of trust might afford the prudent man sufficient safeguards against the improper circulation of his portrait; but since the latest advances in photographic art have rendered it possible to take pictures surreptitiously, the doctrines of contract and of trust are inadequate to support the required protection and the law of tort must be resorted to. The right of property in its widest sense, including all possession, including all rights and privileges, and hence embracing the right to an inviolate personality, affords alone that broad basis upon which the protection which the individual demands can be rested." "Right to Privacy," 211.

16. "The press is overstepping in every direction the obvious bounds of propriety and of decency. Gossip is no longer the resource of the idle and the vicious, but has become a trade which is pursued with industry as well as effrontery. To satisfy a prurient taste the detail of sexual relations are spread broadcast in the columns of the daily papers. To occupy the indolent, column upon column is filled with idle gossip which can only be procured upon intrusion into the domestic circle. The intensity and complexity of life, attendant upon advancing civilization, have rendered necessary some retreat from the world, and man, under the refining influence of culture, has become more sensitive to the publicity, so that solitude and privacy have become more essential to the individual; but modern enterprise and invention have, through invasions upon his privacy, subjected him to mental pain and distress, far greater than could be inflicted by mere bodily injury." Warren and Brandeis, "Right to Privacy," 196.

17. Thomas D. Selz et al., *Entertainment Law: Legal Concepts and Business Practices,* 2nd ed. (St. Paul, MN: Thompson-West, 1996), 21, n. 17.

18. James Q. Whitman, "The Two Western Cultures of Privacy: Dignity versus Liberty," *Yale Law Journal* 113 (2004): 1151, 1209. Whitman explores how, starting

with the famous *Sidis* case of 1940, American law began to favor the interests of the press over almost any claim to privacy.

19. Diane L. Zimmerman, "Requiem for a Heavyweight: A Farewell to Warren and Brandeis's Privacy Tort," *Cornell Law Review* 68 (1983): 291, 362.

20. *Doe v. Millis,* 536 N.W.2d 824 (Mich. Ct. App. 1995).

21. J. Thomas McCarthy, *The Rights of Publicity and Privacy*, 2nd ed. (St. Paul, MN: Thomson-West, 2007) 383.

22. *National Archives and Records Admin. v. Favish,* 541 U.S. 157 (2004).

23. *National Archives and Records Admin.,* 541 U.S. 157 (2004), at 168–69.

24. *Providence Journal Co. v. Town of West Warwick,* No. 03-207, 2004 WL 1770102 (R.I. 22 July 2004). Request for information was brought under the Rhode Island Access to Public Records Act. This case is discussed in Clay Calvert, "The Privacy of Death: An Emergent Jurisprudence and Legal Rebuke to Media Exploitation and a Voyeuristic Culture," *Loyola Law and Entertainment Law Review* 26 (2005–6): 133.

25. *New York Times Co. v. City of New York Fire Dept.,* 829 N.E.2d 266 (2005), brought under NY State FOIA.

26. *Savala v. Freedom Communications, Inc.,* 2006 WL 1738169 (27 June 2006).

27. One philosopher described the problem of posthumous harm as one of the most puzzling: "Plausible and well considered arguments can be presented to support positive or negative answers to these questions. And yet . . . either response to each of these questions may appear, for clear and evident reasons, to be strange and outlandish; in a word, these questions seem to be such that no answer can put us fully at ease." Ernest Partridge, "Posthumous Interests and Posthumous Respect," *Ethics* 91 (1981): 243.

28. Comunicato stampa—04 ottobre 2005, "Il Garante su Franco Scoglio no alle immagini della morte Roma," Rome, 4 October 2005.

29. Comunicato stampa—30 dicembre 2006, "Immagina morte Saddam: dichiarazione di Francesco Pizzetti, Presidente dell'Autorità Garante per la privacy, Roma, 30 dicembre 2006," Provvedimento del 15 luglio 2006 [Formal decision, ex officio, greater force than press release], Rome, 15 July 2006.

30. Provvedimento [Formal decision ex officio, greater force than a Press Release] del 15 luglio 2006, Rome, 15 July 2006.

31. Provvedimento del 11 ottobre 2006, "Il garante per la protezione dei dati personali," Rome, 11 October 2006.

32. *Riley v. St. Louis County of Mo.,* 153 F.3d 627 (1997). Even if the officer's statements about the boy were intentionally false, there would still be no cause of action because of the notion that the dead cannot be defamed.

33. The "general right of personality" has been recognized by the German Bundesgerichtshof, or BGH, Germany's highest court in civil law, since 1954 (permanent jurisdiction since BGHZ 13, 334, 338) both as a fundamental right, constitutionally guaranteed by arts. 1 and 2 of the German constitution and by civil law as a protected "other right" in sec. 823, abs. 1, of the German civil code. Gotz Bottner, "Protection

of the Honour of Deceased Persons: A Comparison between the German and the Australian Legal Situations," *Bond Law Review* 13 (2001): 109.

34. BVerfGE 30, 173.

35. Whitman, "Two Western Cultures of Privacy," 1151, 1211.

36. Tim Arango, "Jackson Earnings Grow by Millions after Death," *New York Times,* 13 August 2009.

37. See *Haelan Lab., Inc., v. Topps Chewing Gum, Inc.,* 202 F.2d 866, 868 (2d Cir. 1953), *cert denied,* 346 U.S. 816 (1953) (the unauthorized use of photographs of prominent baseball players who had previously licensed the exclusive use of their pictures of plaintiffs violated players' "right to publicity"); Jonathan L. Kranz, "Sharing the Spotlight: Equitable Distribution of the Right of Publicity," *Cardozo Arts and Entertainment Law Journal* 13 (1995): 917, 934.

38. *Roberson v. Rochester Folding Box Co.,* 64 N.E. 442 (N.Y. 1902), discussed in McCarthy, *Rights of Publicity,* § 1.16.

39. *Pavesich v. New England Life Insurance,* 50 S.E. 68 (Ga. 1905).

40. *Haelan Lab.,* 202 F.2d at 866.

41. See *Haelan Lab.,* 202 F.2d at 868; and Kenneth E. Spahn, "The Right of Publicity: A Matter of Privacy, Property, or Public Domain?" *Nova Law Review* 19 (1995): 1013, 1023.

42. As one commentator noted: "It may seem surprising to the casual observer that Indiana is the home of the most comprehensive Right of Publicity statute in the United States. Since the elusive Right of Publicity is usually only implicated in high-profile celebrity lawsuits, intuition suggests that such a distinction might belong to California or New York. After all, the entertainment industry is concentrated in Los Angeles and New York City, and a significant percentage of celebrities are domiciliaries of California and New York. Nevertheless, by virtue of the 1994 addition to the Indiana Code, as embodied in §§ 32-13-1-1 through 32-13-1-20, the distinction of having the most progressive publicity statute in the nation belongs to Indiana." Jonathan L. Faber, "Indiana: A Celebrity-Friendly Jurisdiction," *Res Gestae* 43 (2000): 24–30.

43. Rosemary Coombe, "Authorizing the Celebrity: Publicity Rights, Postmodern Politics, and Unauthorized Genders," *Cardozo Arts and Entertainment Law Journal* 10 (1992): 365, 366–67.

44. *Carson v. Here's Johnny Portable Toilets, Inc.,* 698 F.2d 831 (6th Cir. 1983); *White v. Samsung Electronics America, Inc.,* 989 F.2d 1512 (9th Cir. 1993); *Midler v. Ford Motor Co.,* 849 F.2d 460 (9th Cir. 1988); *Onassis v. Christian Dior–New York, Inc.,* 472 N.Y.S.2d 254 (N.Y. Sup. Ct. 1984).

45. Although some early cases suggested that the right to publicity should survive death only if the right was commercially exploited during life, this limitation has not been explicitly adopted by courts or legislatures.

46. McCarthy, *Rights of Publicity,* § 9.18.

47. McCarthy, *Rights of Publicity,* § 9.19.

48. McCarthy, *Rights of Publicity,* § 9.16–40.

49. Michael Madow, "Private Ownership of Public Image: Popular Culture and

Publicity Rights," *California Law Review* 81 (1993): 125, 132. CKX, Inc., also owns the rights to Muhammad Ali through its subsidiary G.O.A.T., LLC. G.O.A.T. stands for "Greatest of All Time," a registered trademark of G.O.A.T., LLC. Does this mean that no one in the future can ever surpass Ali as the greatest of all time? Or if they do, they cannot proclaim that it is so?

50. Mark McKenna, "The Right of Publicity and Autonomous Self-Definition," *University of Pittsburgh Law Review* 67 (2005–6): 225, 253.

51. Coombe, "Authorizing the Celebrity," 370–71.

52. Coombe, "Authorizing the Celebrity," 370–71.

53. David Lange, "Recognizing the Public Domain," *Law and Contemporary Problems* 44 (1981): 147, 163.

54. Anthony Liebig, "Style and Performance," *Bulletin of the Copyright Society* 17 (1969): 40, 47, quoted in Lange, "Reimagining the Public Domain," 463, 467.

55. Madow, "Private Ownership of Public Image," 145.

56. Ray D. Madoff, "Taxing Personhood: Estate Taxes and the Compelled Commodification of Identity," *Virginia Tax Review* 17 (1998): 759; Mitchell M. Gans, Bridget J. Crawford, and Jonathan G. Blattmachr, "The Estate Tax Fundamentals of Celebrity and Control," *Yale Law Journal* 118 (2008): Pocket Part 50; Joshua C. Tate, "Marilyn Monroe's Legacy: Taxation of Postmortem Publicity Rights," *Yale Law Journal* 118 (2008): Pocket Part 38.

57. With the possibility of renewal for another fourteen years if the writer was still living at the expiration of the first term.

58. James Casner and W. Barton, *Leach Cases and Text on Property,* 4th ed. (New York: Aspen Law and Business, 2000), 211.

59. The only requirement is that the expression be in a form that is tangible and fixed. A dance or performance style can meet this requirement by videotaping.

60. There are no quality standards for copyright; we are all creating copyrighted material many times a day. However, the law of copyright has practical effect only in those areas where there is public interest in the work.

61. In England this "right to copy" books was originally granted to publishers and not authors. It was a government-authorized monopoly given to the operators of the printing press. The right did not become a right of the author until the Statute of Anne in 1710. Marci Hamilton, *The Historical and Philosophical Underpinnings of the Copyright Clause,* Occasional Papers in Intellectual Property from the Benjamin N. Cardozo School of Law Yeshiva University (New York: Benjamin N. Cardozo School of Law, Yeshiva University, Jacob Burns Institute for Advanced Legal Studies, 1999).

62. U.S. Constitution, art. 1, sec. 8, cl. 8.

63. Paul K. Saint-Armour, *The Copywrights: Intellectual Property and the Literary Imagination* (Ithaca, NY: Cornell University Press, 2003), 125. He estimated that nineteen years would be optimal. The first copyright statute provided for a term of fourteen years with the possibility of renewing for one additional fourteen-year term.

64. *Eldred v. Ashcroft,* 537 U.S. 186 (2003).

65. *Arguments before the Committees on Patents of the Senate and House of Representatives, Conjointly, on S. 6330 and H.R. 19853,* 59th Cong. at 116–21 (1906) (statement of Samuel L. Clemens). Clemens's testimony is reprinted in its entirety in Samuel L. Clemens, "Copyright in Perpetuity," *Green Bag,* 2nd ser., 6, no. 1 (2002): 109, quotation at 111 (original testimony referenced in n. 1). Of course, at the time of Clemens's testimony, the life of a book depended heavily on a publisher's willingness to invest capital in publishing the work. (Indeed, one of Clemens's concerns with limiting the term of copyright was that upon the expiration of the copyright term, several publishers would flood the market with cheap editions, the result being none of them could make enough profit to sustain production over time.) "Copyright in Perpetuity," n. 3. However, in the twenty-first century, when information is easily stored and transmitted electronically, the balance may be different.

In England, William Wordsworth similarly led the charge to extend copyright protection. See Susan Eilenberg, "Mortal Pages: Wordsworth and the Reform for Copyright," *ELH* 56 (1989): 351–74.

66. D. T. Max, "The Injustice Collector," *New Yorker,* 19 June 2006.

67. Saint-Armour, *Copywrights,* 156.

68. Saint-Armour, *Copywrights,* 157.

69. Mark Rose, *Authors and Owners: The Invention of Copyright* (Cambridge, MA: Harvard University Press, 1993), 2.

70. Paul M. Schwartz and William Michael Treanor, "Eldred and Lochner: Copyright Term Extension and the Intellectual Property as Constitutional Property," *Yale Law Journal* 112 (2001): 2331, 2338.

71. "'Gone with the Wind' Parody Draws Challenges, Supporters," *CNNfyi.com,* 13 April 2001, available at: http://archives.cnn.com/2001/fyi/news/04/13/wind.done.gone/.

72. Rose, *Authors and Owners,* 2.

73. Rose, *Authors and Owners,* 2.

74. See Alfred Yen, "Eldred, the First Amendment, and Aggressive Copyright Claims," *Houston Law Review* 40 (2003): 673, 675, and articles cited in n. 5.

75. Joe Liu, "Copyright and Breathing Space," *Columbia Journal of Law and the Arts* 30 (2007): 429.

76. Liu, "Copyright and Breathing Space." The fair use exception provides: "Notwithstanding the provisions of sections 106 and 106A, the fair use of a copyrighted work, including such use by reproduction in copies or phonorecords or by any other means specified by that section, for purposes such as criticism, comment, news reporting, teaching (including multiple copies for classroom use), scholarship, or research, is not an infringement of copyright." 17 U.S.C. 107.

77. David Nimmer, "'Fairest of Them All' and Other Fairy Tales of Fair Use," *Law and Contemporary Problems* 66 (2003): 263, 281–82.

78. Liu, "Copyright and Breathing Space," 106 and articles cited in n. 27.

79. Joseph P. Liu, "Copyright and Time: A Proposal," *Michigan Law Review* 101 (2002): 409; Justin Hughes, "Fair Use across Time," *UCLA Law Review* 50 (2003):

775; Michael W. Carroll, "Fixing Fair Use," *North Carolina Law Review* 85 (2007): 1087; Gideon Parchomovsky and Kevin A. Goldman, "Fair Use Harbors," *Virginia Law Review* 93 (2007): 1483.

80. *Geisel v. Poynter Products, Inc.*, 295 F. Supp. 331 (S.D.N.Y. 1968). Today some limited relief could be provided by 17 U.S.C. § 203 (2002), which gives artists a limited window in which to reclaim their copyright interest.

81. Cambra E. Stern, "A Matter of Life or Death: The Visual Artists Rights Act and the Problem of Postmortem Moral Rights," *UCLA Law Review* 51 (2004): 849, 854.

82. In C. Van Rij and H. Best, eds., *Moral Rights: Reports Presented at the Meeting of the International Association of Entertainment Lawyers, MIDEM 1995, Cannes* (Apeldoorn, Netherlands: MAKLU, 1995), 27–36.

Conclusion

1. Zygmunt Bauman, *Mortality, Immortality and Other Life Strategies* (Stanford, CA: Stanford University Press, 1992). Determining who has been given particularized immortality is best understood by studying what is done rather than what is said. Consider the Gettysburg Address. President Abraham Lincoln spoke the words: "The world will little note, nor long remember what we say here, but it can never forget what they did here." And yet, 150 years later, Lincoln is regarded as one of our greatest presidents, with his speech regularly recited and memorized by millions, but few could answer the question, "What happened at the Battle of Gettysburg?" let alone name one soldier who fought there.

2. Arnold Toynbee, "Changing Attitudes towards Death in the Modern Western World," in *Man's Concern with Death*, ed. Arnold Toynbee et al. (New York: McGraw-Hill, 1968), 131.

INDEX